Brian Cain's 4RIP3 Softball Mental Conditioning Program

MASTERS OF THE MENTAL GAME SERIES BOOK

This book is being given to

Makenzie

because I care about you and your success

Brian M. Cain, MS, CMAA
Brian Cain Peak Performance, LLC

What Champions Are Saying About Brian Cain & The 4RIP3 Softball Mental Conditioning Program

"Absolutely fantastic! Really took practical information and made it applicable to our program athletes and staff."

**Nate Parsley
Rowan University**

"Great job, Brian! I love this 4RIP3 program. It makes coaching the mental game so much easier."

**Tina Deese
Auburn University**

"Brian is a great presenter who has tremendous energy and has a very practical, use-it-today method that coaches can use immediately."

**John Tschida
University of St. Thomas**

"Using the 4RIP3 program once a day as part of our reconnection routine in January has played a huge difference in our success."

**Lucy Bass
University of Alabama, Birmingham**

"AWESOME!!! Brian Cain has done it again. This is going to change the game of softball."

**Craig Snider
Florida State University**

Brian Cain's 4RIP3 Softball Mental Conditioning Program

Brian M. Cain, MS, CMAA

Brian Cain Peak Performance, LLC

Brian M. Cain, MS, CMAA
Peak Performance Coach
Peak Performance Publishing
Brian Cain Peak Performance, LLC

Brian Cain's 4RIP3 Softball Mental Conditioning Program

A Masters of the Mental Game Series Book
©2013 by Brian M. Cain, MS, CMAA

All rights reserved. No part of this book may be reproduced, stored in a retrieval system, or transmitted in any form or by any means (electronic, mechanical, photocopying, recording, or by any information retrieval system, or otherwise) without the prior express written consent of the author and Peak Performance Publishing, except for the inclusion of brief quotations in critical articles or a review.

Printed in the United States of America
Edited by: Mary Lou Schueler
Cover design & book layout: Daniel Yeager
Illustrations: Nicole Ludwig and Greg Pajala
Photography: Don Whipple and Paul Lamontangue

Brian M. Cain, MS, CMAA

Brian Cain's 4RIP3 Softball Mental Conditioning Program

A Masters of the Mental Game Series Book
Brian M. Cain, MS, CMAA
p. cm.

CONTENTS

What Champions Are Saying About
Brian Cain & The 4Rip3 Softball
Mental Conditioning Program II

Introduction 1

**01. Introduction To Cain, 4Rip3
And Mental Conditioning
For Softball** 3
Start Fast And Finish Strong 3
I Wish I Had This Back Then 4
My Competitive Advantage Is Yours 5
Meeting Mike Candrea 5
The System Has Been Passed On 6
The Game Knows 6
4 Stages Of Commitment 6
A Woman On A Mission 7
What Is Your Why? 8
Why Do You Play Softball? 9
3 Steps To Performance Improvement 10
Goal Of 4Rip3 Program 10
Goal Must Be In Your Control 11
Training Vs. Practice Mentality 11
Acronyms Are Easy To Remember 11
Three Things To Do On A Daily Basis 12
Review Sheet 13

**02. Making 4Rip3 Your Mission
And Memorizing Anything** 17
Your Mission For Today 18
4 Stages Of Acceptance 19
Trained Or Untrained Memory 20
3 Steps To Memorize Anything 20
The 10 Locations Of Skeleton Files 21
Painting Pictures On The Locations 22
Location 1 – Compete In The Present 22

Check For Understanding 22
Location 2 – Stick To The Process 23
Review 23
Location 3 – Control What You Can 23
Review 24
Location 4 – Be Positive 24
Turn Have To Into Want To 25
I Can't Do It Yet 25
Compared To What 25
Gratitude And Happiness 26
Winners And Learners 26
Review 27
Location 5 – Mental Imagery 27
Pillow And Potty Training 27
Review 28
Location 6 - Routines 28
Review 29
Location 7 – Recognize Your Signals 29
Location 8 – Release / Flush It 30
Location 9 – Refocus On The Next Pitch 30
Location 10 – Dominate The Day 31
Review 31
Congratulations 32
Review At Practice Each Day With Team 32
Review Sheet 34

03. Compete In The Present Moment
   One Pitch At A Time 37
Skeleton File System Review 37
Each Pitch Has A Life And History 38
Compete In The Present Moment 38
Spend Vs. Invest Time 39
Invest Your $86,400 40
How Do You Define Success? 40
How To Get In The Present 41
Three Major Exercises 41
The Breath In Softball 42

Concentration Grids 42
5-4-3-2-1 Breathing Exercise 44
5-4-3-2-1 Breathing Exercise Script 44
Reflection On Exercise 45
Inhale & Exhale Exercise 46
Inhale & Exhale Exercise Script 46
Inhale & Exhale Exercise Reflection 47

04. Focus On The Process Over The Outcome 51
Process Over Outcome Approach 51
4Rip3 Review 51
Control What You Can Control 52
The Staircase To Your Goals 52
Walk The Staircase One Step At A Time 52
The Law Of Averages 53
Seven Ways To Beat The Game 54
No Errors 54
Score First 54
Two Out Of Three For A Strike 54
Give Up 3 Runs Or Less 55
54% Quality At-Bats 55
Score 5 Runs Or More 55
Win The Free Base – Freebie War 56
Seven Ways To Beat Game Review 56
Know Your Mission 56
Control What You Can Control 57
What You Can Control 59
What You Can't Control 59
You Can't Control Winning 59
The Zone Does Not Exist 60
Confidence 60
Even The Best Focus Is Wrong
At Times 61
Review Sheet 62

05. Staying Positive In A Game Of Failure 65
Stay Positive In A Game Of Failure 65
What Do Positive Players Do? 65
No Pink Elephants – Pictures Win 66
Focus On What You Want 66
Amazing Story Of Belief & Barriers 66
Why Eat Fire? 68
Attitude Of Gratitude 68
Compared To What 68
Perspective Posters 69
The Voice Of Self-Talk 69
Green Means Go 69
Train Your Wolf 69
Iphone Confidence Conditioning 70
E + R = O In Softball 71
Will Beats Skill 71
The Confidence Resume 71
The Big Abc's 71
Review Sheeet 73

06. Mental Imagery
For Softball Performance 75
Mental Imagery For Softball 75
You Do Imagery Without Knowing It 75
Highlight Videos Help 76
Relaxation & Using Senses Help 76
Thinking About Softball Vs. Imagery 76
Why Is Mental Imagery Effective? 77
Four Steps To Mental Imagery 77
Coaches, Take Notice 78
Passive Vs. Active Imagery 78
Coaches, Make This Part Of The Routine 79
Mental Imagery For Softball Script 79
Part 1 – Relaxation Training 80
Part 2 – Confidence Conditioning 81
Part 3 – Mental Recall 82
Part 4 – Mental Rehearsal 82

Concluding Your Imagery Session...........................84

07. Establishing Routines For Consistent Softball Performance 87
A Wise Man Speaks – Good To Great....................87
Why Are Routines Important? 87
What Does A Routine Look Like?..........................88
Examples Of Routines..88
Change Your Clothes & Mentality 88
Use The Shoes 89
Shower It Off 90
Important To Have Post-Game Routine 90
Video Resources For You 90
When The At-Bat Starts 90
Use A Release 91
Visualize The Hourglass Routine 93
Circle Of Focus 93
Three Components Of A Routine 93
Deep Breath..93
Final Thought...94
Release 94
What Do You Do When Not Playing? 95
Taking Mental Reps 95
Superstition Vs. Routine......................................96
Trust Your Routines...97
Review Sheet 98

08. Recognizing Your Signal Lights Go Green 101
Recognition Is Essential For Success 101
Grab The Wheel And Hold On.............................101
We Live In Yellow Lights 101
Awareness And Control 102
Masters Of The Mental Game..............................102
Examples Of Signal Lights 103
Good & Bad, Never Good Or Bad 104
Prayer, Primal, Perfect..105
Can't Walk On Water 106

Check In 106
Atw – Awareness To Win 107
Review Sheet 108

09. Release Your Mental Bricks & Refocus On Win So What, Next Pitch! 111

4Rip3 Review 111
Release And Refocus 112
Examples Of Releases 112
Pre-Determined Release 113
So What 113
Examples Of Releases 114
Release Focal Points 114
Releases For Hitters 114
Releases For Pitchers 114
Releases For Defense 115
Post-Practice Release 115
Mental Bricks 115
Be Coachable 116
Personal Attack Vs. Professional Coach 116
Recognizing Green Vs. Red 117
The 4Rip3 System 117
Review Sheet 118

10. The Compound Effect, Tying It All Together And Getting To Work 121

This Is The Start, Not The End 121
The Compound Effect 121
Water The Bamboo 122
You Just Never Know 122
Avoid Cam's Mistake 123
Cam's Mistake 123
The Start Stops Most People 123
4Rip3 Review 124
Review Sheet 135

**Sample Chapter From
Cain's Book Champions Tell All**.................... **149**
   Sample Chapter 151
   When To Focus On One Sport 151
   Finding The College Of Your Choice 151
   College Sports Can Be A Rude Awakening 152
   Fails For First Time 152
   Fresh Start, Same Challenges 153
   Another Year, Another Struggle 153
   Key To Unlocking Potential Is Found 153
   Unique Style – Finding Out Who
   You Need To Be 154
   Ah Ha Moment 154
   Regrets & Expensive Experience 155
   Talent Is Overrated 155
   Analysis Paralysis 156
   Perfectionism Kills Performance 156
   Routine Helps Set Pace 156
   Change Self Talk, Change Your Life 157
   Green Shoelaces 157
   Use The Shoelace As A Release 158
   Senior Year = Totally Different Pitcher 158
   Separating Life As Person And Competitor 159
   Softball Is Not Life And Death 159
   The Perfectionist Test 160
   Focal Points Help To Refocus 161
   Sport Specialization 162
   Do You Pick Sport, Or Does Sport Pick You? 163
   Mental Imagery Plays Large Role In Preparation .. 163
   Recognizing Your Signal Lights 165
   Awareness Is The First Step To Accomplishment .. 165
   So What Next Pitch Mentality 167
   Mental Game Extends Into Life After Softball 168
   Antidote For The Grind Of Everyday Work 168
   Dominate The Day 169
   Sport Does Not Define You 169
   Amanda Crabtree Review 170

Sample Chapter From Cain's Book
So What, Next Pitch! **173**
    National Championship Mental Conditioning
    Alabama's Patrick Murphy 174
    Sharing Of Articles A Success 176
    Characteristics Of A Great Leader 179
    Core Covenants Are Key 178
    Foundations Of Success 179

How You Can Become
A Master Of The Mental Game...................... **183**

Who Is Brian M. Cain, MS, CMAA
Peak Performance Coach **187**

Concentration Grids **189**

Notes Pages.. **199**

INTRODUCTION
READ THIS FIRST

Softball is quite possibly the most mentally demanding game in the world. When it comes to performing at your best when it means the most on the diamond, it is as much about the six inches between your ears as it is the six feet below them.

I have worked with many of the top college and high school softball programs in the country, as well as with the elite of Mixed Martial Arts, the Olympics, the NFL, NHL and in Major League Baseball - and they have all confirmed that as they climb higher and higher in the levels of competition, success becomes less about physical skills and more about the mental game, because at the highest level everyone has the physical skills to be successful.

The softball players who achieve greatness are the ones that have the mental skills to perform consistently at or near their best. In my 4RIP3 Softball Mental Conditioning Program I take you through the essential steps to developing mental toughness. This is the same program I take the top college programs through each year.

You have three audio CDs and this accompanying manual to help you master the mental game. This is a manual, not a book. This is a transcription of the audio program to provide an easy-to-follow text version of the information presented. If you just read this book and do not listen to the audios, this may not make 100% sense. You must use the two in conjunction. My suggestion is that you listen to the audio chapter and then read the book, as it will help to reinforce what you have learned and will also serve as a quality set of reminders and a great reference for you to come back to.

Each chapter has a review section at the end that you should fill out as you listen to the audio or as you go through the text.

Thank you again for your investment into the mental game of softball. If you are interested in bringing my Winners Workshop or Peak Performance Bootcamp to your softball program, team or organization, please visit www.briancain.com for more information.

Brian M. Cain, MS, CMAA

Peak Performance Expert In Softball

Softball's Premier Mental Conditioning Coach

INTRODUCTION TO CAIN, 4RIP3 AND MENTAL CONDITIONING FOR SOFTBALL

This is Brian Cain, your Peak Performance and Mental Conditioning Coach with 4RIP3 Softball, your Mental Toughness and Mental Conditioning Training System for Peak Performance Softball. In this 10-audio series, I will take you through the proven system I have used that has helped to win state and national championships in the game of softball and has helped countless coaches, players and programs to perform at their best when it means the most.

Softball is possibly the greatest mental game that there is. There's more failure in the game of softball than in any other game. And yes, there's more softball in failure than baseball. Sorry, guys. You see, the game of softball happens so fast - it's such a short game. You make one mistake, and the next thing you know everything caves in. You've been there. You've been suffocated by the pressure before, suffocated by the failure that is built into this great game.

My mission, through the 4RIP3 Softball Mental Conditioning Program, is to train you on how you can play your best when it means the most in the game of softball. Before we get into exactly what the 4RIP3 System is, let's understand that you're already a winner. The reason why you're already a winner and already a champion is that it's the start that stops most people, and you have gotten started with audio #1. Congratulations!

START FAST AND FINISH STRONG

Now, if you want to be world-class, if you want to be at the highest level of softball, you can't just start fast and get all into it with this first audio. You've got to finish strong and make it all the way to the end.

You can go through all ten audios in one day or through ten audios in ten days or ten audios over ten weeks. There are many ways to "eat that frog," as Stephen Covey would say. You've just got to find out what way is going to work for you because this program is about you – you reaching your true potential in the game of softball, you learning how to better play one pitch at a time, you learning how to become a master of the mental game. My suggestion is to go through ten audios in ten straight days and then listen to one a week or more if your schedule and commitment to excellence permit.

I WISH I HAD THIS BACK THEN

As a college baseball player at the University of Vermont, I went in with tremendous expectations for myself. I went in wanting to be the number one pitcher. My freshman year, I had a big scholarship that I had to live up to - well, that I wanted to live up to. And needless to say, my college baseball career was a complete failure. I couldn't get anybody out. I didn't get the innings I wanted. I didn't help my team succeed. But through that failure, I learned many things that got me to Cal State Fullerton, where I was a college baseball graduate assistant coach doing my Master's degree in sports psychology with the legend in the mental game of softball, Dr. Ken Ravizza.

I had the best of both worlds. I learned in the classroom about the mental game from Dr. Ravizza and got to see how the Cal State Fullerton baseball and softball programs would apply what he was teaching. The coaches and players were tremendous. It was a life-changing experience for me, to say the least.

Dr. Ravizza's philosophies and teachings on the mental game allowed me the most unique experience any peak performance and mental conditioning coach has ever had. Not only did I learn from the greatest sports psychology instructor, Ken Ravizza, on the planet, I saw as a baseball coach how his skills were applied in two of the top college programs in the country.

MY COMPETITIVE ADVANTAGE IS YOURS

I think that's the competitive advantage that I give you. I see myself as more of a mental conditioning and peak performance coach than I do a psychologist because I don't want you to lie down on a couch and tell me about your feelings and tell me about what's going on in your world. I want you to perform at your best regardless of how you feel because there are going to be days in softball – let's face it – where you don't feel good. You're actually going to feel like garbage, and you still have to go perform because softball success is about action. It's not about feeling. Feelings will lie to you. Actions will get you results.

MEETING MIKE CANDREA

I remember being at graduate school, standing there with Dr. Ravizza when he was having a conversation with Mike Candrea, the ultra-successful softball coach at the University of Arizona. And Ken said: "Brian, are there any questions you want to ask Mike? He's one of the best coaches in softball history. What questions do you have for him?"

And I said: "Coach Candrea, I didn't realize you had coached baseball at a very high level at Central Arizona Community College, one of the top baseball programs in the county, before you were coaching softball at Arizona. What's the difference between coaching men at the highest level in baseball and women in the highest level in softball?"

He responded: "Brian, it's real simple. Guys have to play well to feel good. Women have to feel good to play well. Coaching guys is about an ego; coaching women is about emotion." And then, pointing at Dr. Ravizza, he said: "What the mental game does, what his system has allowed us to do is take some of that emotion out of the game and get our athletes to act differently than how they feel. You know, to fake it 'til they make it. So we feel like we have a competitive advantage every time we go out there because we have a skill set to handle that emotion of the game better than the team in the other dugout." And I don't think you can argue with Coach Candrea's results.

THE SYSTEM HAS BEEN PASSED ON

So I want to teach you, as a product of that system, how exactly you can go out, minimize the emotion and maximize the performance. You see, mental toughness is a skill. And it helps you to be at your best when it means the most. And it means the most every single day. Championship softball players don't count the days - they make the days count. Let me say that again. Championship softball players don't count the days - they make the days count. They realize that today plus today plus today equals their softball career. That's right. Your results and your success are the sum of your todays.

THE GAME KNOWS

You see, the game of softball is bigger than us all. Without the game of softball you and I would have never crossed paths. You would not be listening to this audio, and you would not have all the great teammates that you do today. And the game of softball - it knows. The game knows, and the game is bigger than us all. And the game will reward those who know why they do what they do. You see, you have to have a big reason why. You've got to know why you play this great game because it's going to be full of adversity.

4 STAGES OF COMMITMENT

There are four stages of commitment to this game: Those who see softball as a job, those who see it as work, those who see it as a potential career and those who are on a mission. You've got to get to the level of mission. And what makes it a mission? A mission is that for every single day you wake up you have a goal and a purpose for that day. You are a woman on a mission with a purpose, with a goal of what you want to accomplish.

A WOMAN ON A MISSION

Let me tell you about a woman on a mission. A few years ago I'm in Dallas, Texas - Strong Man Competition at the Dallas County Fair. A man's on stage ripping phone books in half; rolling up frying pans to make them look like burritos; taking a deck of cards, ripping it in half; taking a crowbar and just bending it in half. I've never seen anything like it.

He grabs a lemon, and he grabs a cup in his other hand. And he says to the audience: "I am the world's strongest man. You've seen me rip phone books and bend a crowbar in half. In my final test of strength, I will open up a competition to anyone in the stands. I will squeeze all the juice out of this lemon. And if you want to come down and try to squeeze another drop out of the lemon, I will give you $1,000."

All of a sudden these two huge Dallas Cowboy-looking guys come up on stage. They grab the lemon after it's been wrung out by the strong man. They grab the lemon, they grab the cup and they squeeze - and nothing happens. Everyone in the crowd starts laughing.

And the strong man was about to go on with his presentation, proving to everyone that you could not get one extra drop of juice out of that lemon, until a woman came walking up from the back of the crowd. She had a cane in her right hand, had long gray hair, and kind of limped towards the stage as a hush came over the crowd. And the strong man said: "Ma'am, I'm sorry. I know we have opened up this competition to anyone, but you saw that the two Dallas Cowboy-looking players couldn't get the drop of juice out of the lemon. Do you really think you can get a drop out of that lemon?She got on stage, looked at the man, and said: "Sir. Please. Just give me a chance. Just give me a chance." "Well, Ma'am, we're here to give everyone a chance today. Here's the lemon. Here's the cup. Let's see what you can do. But make it quick." And the woman grabbed the lemon, grabbed the cup. And with all her might, body just trembling, glasses falling off of her head, veins popping out...

Boom! All of a sudden, a drop of juice came out of the lemon into the glass. And the crowd erupted. And the strong man said: "Ma'am, I've never, ever seen anyone get a drop of juice out of the lemon. How did you do it?" And she said: "Sir, my husband just lost his job. We've got five grandchildren living with us. And I really needed that $1,000 to feed my grandchildren."

WHAT IS YOUR WHY?

You see, the woman had a "why." She had a big reason why. And when you have a big enough reason why, you will always, always find a way "how." So what is your "why"? Why do you play the game of softball? That's the question you have to ask yourself. And that's the question that you want to discuss together in your group today: Why do you play the game of softball?

WHY DO YOU PLAY SOFTBALL?

3 STEPS TO PERFORMANCE IMPROVEMENT

If you want to find a way "how" to take your performance to the next level, it's really easy. There are three steps to performance improvement that were taught to me by a legend in the field of mental conditioning, Harvey Dorfman. He wrote the books *The Mental Game of Baseball, The Mental ABC's of Pitching,* and *The Mental Keys to Hitting.* If you enjoy reading, I'd highly suggest checking those books out as well as Dr. Ravizza's book, *Heads-Up Baseball* and, of course, the five that I've written: *Toilets, Bricks, Fish Hooks and PRIDE; So What, Next Pitch!; The Mental Conditioning Manual; Champions Tell All;* and *The Daily Dominator.*

The three steps to performance improvement taught by Harvey Dorman were:

      1. Awareness
      2. Strategy
      3. Action

How do you build awareness? You've got to ask yourself: "On a scale of one to ten, how would I grade myself right now compared to where I want to be?" And whether you give yourself a two, a three, an eight or a seven, then create strategies by saying, "What's one thing I should start doing, one thing I should stop doing and one thing I should continue doing to help me move closer towards a ten?" Then put those strategies into action. You see, if you do those, you will create the way "how" to achieve your "why." But you must start with your "why."

GOAL OF 4RIP3 PROGRAM

The goal of the 4RIP3 Softball Mental Conditioning Program is to help you play one pitch at a time and know that the process of who you become, by listening to these audios, is more important than the end results that you get on the field because, through that process of becoming more, you will achieve more on the field.

GOAL MUST BE IN YOUR CONTROL

And a statement that you'll hear us say a lot through this audio is that your goal must, absolutely must, be in your control. And you have control over the process of who you become, of how you work, of what you focus on. You don't have control of the outcome of how you play softball. There are just too many factors. So you must keep your goal within your control, and that's a goal that is based on the process. You see, mentally tough athletes focus on what they want – not what they're trying to avoid. And in softball, the best team never wins. It's always the team that plays the best.

TRAINING VS. PRACTICE MENTALITY

We'll talk a lot about increasing the quality of your practice, the quality of your training. I will talk a lot about softball practice. I will call it softball training. Why? Because elite, special operations, special force warriors like Navy Seals don't practice. They train. They train because they're on a mission. And they train because they know practice and training don't make perfect. They make permanent. So how you train, how you compete on a daily basis in your "training/practice" is going to show up every day on the field because practice makes permanent.

ACRONYMS ARE EASY TO REMEMBER

Let's talk about the 4RIP3 System. It's an acronym. Acronyms are easy to help you remember things. In our next audio, we'll teach you exactly how to remember what the 4RIP3 System is.

The four R's: Routine, recognize, release, refocus. The "I" is mental imagery. And the three P's are to live in the present, focus on the process and stay positive.

When you work the 4RIP3 System, you'll improve the quality of your training. And that step-up that we try to often do in big games, which often leads to a failure, is going to happen every day. You see, when you step up every day then there is no step-up. The key in all of this is that you take great notes, you review your notes, you live your notes. And you know that in order to improve, you have to do a little a lot – not a lot a little. You must totally immerse yourself into this process.

THREE THINGS TO DO ON A DAILY BASIS

So here are three things I want you to do. I want you to read my Daily Dominator message. *The Daily Dominator* is a book that I wrote with 366 days - that's right, 366 days, because it might be a leap year - of one-page-a-day reads to help you have that internal GPS that's going to reroute you back to where you want to be between the ears.

For example, if we were taking off from Burlington, Vermont, where I currently live, to Oklahoma City for the Women's College World Series and we were to fly all the way there, that plane would be off course 98% of the time. But what a GPS does is to make us land where we want to land, to always make sure we execute our mission. And *The Daily Dominator* helps you, day by day, to create the mentality that you want. Reading *The Daily Dominator* is like lifting weights for your brain and your mental toughness.

The other thing I want you to do is go to www.briancain.com/monday and sign up for my Monday VIP e-mail message. I want you to get my Monday message and hear from me directly every single week, then listen to these 4RIP3 audios and review your notes. This process will help you to develop the mindset and become the person that you need to become to play your best when it means the most, which is every single day, and allow you to dominate the day every day you play softball.

Introduction to Cain, 4RIP3 and Mental Conditioning for Softball

REVIEW SHEET

1. It is the _____ that _____ most people.

2. Where did Cain play college baseball? _____

3. Where did he coach? _____

4. Mental toughness _____ and helps you to be at your _____ when it means the _____.

5. The game of softball _____ and the game is bigger _____.

6. Have a BIG reason _____ and you will find a way _____ (the Lemon Story).

7. Three steps to performance improvement taught to Brian Cain by _____:

    (1) A   1-10 How would you grade yourself? _____

    (2) S   Start: Stop:

    Continue:

    (3) A   7. The goal of the 4RIP3 System is to help you play _____.

8. Know that the _____ is more important than the end result.

9. Your goal must be in your _____. You have control of the _____, not the outcome.

10. Mentally tough athletes focus on what they _____ _____.

11. The best team never wins_____.

12. Practice makes permanent and changes softball practice into softball _____.

13. Four Stages of Commitment:

    (1) J
    (2) W
    (3) C
    (4) M

14. Have a mission for each day (GOAL) and a _____ (PLAN) for each day.

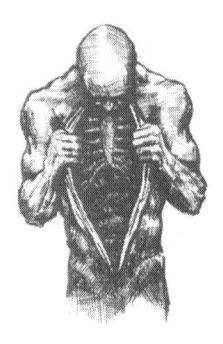

Cain's 4_ _ _ 3 System for Training Mental Toughness in Softball

R1 = R _____

R2 = R _____

R3 = R _____

R4 = R _____

I = _____

P1 = _____

P2 = _____

P3 = _____

15. When you have _____ practice and step up every day, there is no step-up.

16. The key to learning is to totally immerse yourself and do a little _____, not a lot _____.

17. Read or listen to Cain's (1) *Daily Dominator message*, *(2) Monday e-mail, (3) these audios.*

MAKING 4RIP3 YOUR MISSION AND MEMORIZING ANYTHING

Let's review what we learned in the introduction to 4RIP3 and mental conditioning that we covered in audio one.

We learned that it was the start that stops most people.

We know that mental toughness is a skill that helps you to be at your best when it means the most.

We know that the game knows. And the game is bigger than us all and the game will reward those softball players that deserve to win – not the ones who just sit around and talk about how much they want to win - the ones that go out and do the work, the ones that go out and put the principles that you're learning into action, the ones who have a really big reason why. And if you have that big reason "why," you will find the way "how." Remember that lemon story and the woman who won all the money?

We learned the three steps to performance improvement taught to me by one of the great masters of the mental game, Harvey Dorfman, where he said, "All you have is awareness, a strategy and action." You develop awareness by asking yourself, on a scale of one to ten, "Where am I?" And you develop strategy by asking yourself, "What's one thing I need to start, stop and continue to help me get to where I want to be?" And then, you've got to put those strategies into action.

We know that the goal of the 4RIP3 System is to help you play one pitch at a time, and please understand that the process is more important than the end result. Who you become in the process of going through this 4RIP3 System is more important than any one softball game that you win.

I can tell you that you will win more because you will become more. We know that if you want more, you must become more and know that your goal must absolutely, positively be within in your control.

We know that you have control of the process – not the outcome.

We know that mentally tough athletes focus on what they want to do – not what they're trying to avoid - and that the best team never wins. It's always the team that plays the best.

We know that practice makes permanent and that we want to turn a softball practice mentality into a softball training mentality.

We know the four steps of commitment:
1. Having a job
2. Going to work
3. Having a career
4. Being on a mission

My goal is to help you to be on a mission. And when you're on a mission, you have a goal and a purpose for every day; you have quality practice every day so there's no step-up in the game because a step-up happens every single day.

Finally we learned that to become a master of the mental game you must totally immerse yourself into doing a little a lot – not a lot a little.

YOUR MISSION FOR TODAY

Today, as you read this, know that our mission is to teach you about how to memorize anything. You see, you can memorize absolutely anything if you know the four stages of commitment, that this isn't a job, this isn't work, this isn't a career. You are on a mission today to learn how to memorize the 4RIP3 System and all its components so that as we move forward with the next eight audios you will already know what we are learning together.

Now if you don't use this memorization system, you know what happens. If you don't use it, you lose it.

4 STAGES OF ACCEPTANCE

So let's talk about the four stages of acceptance because everyone in the room (whether you're listening to this with your team or you're listening to this on your own) is at one of the four stages of acceptance.

Every softball player I've ever worked with starts off in one of the four stages of acceptance and progresses to stage four by the end of the program. Most softball players start off in stage one and say, "The mental game? This ain't for me." Then they go through it and realize that some of the softball programs that we've worked with have been successful: The University of Alabama won the National Championship in 2012. Four teams went to the NCAA Super Regionals in 2013.

I have a chance to work with some of the greatest softball programs in the country – UAB, Mississippi State, Houston, Arizona State, Coastal Carolina, Maryland, NC State, Georgia, Texas A&M, Auburn, Oregon and all of the top programs in the country are using this same audio training program that you are.

So you may now be saying, "Hey, you know what? This is OK for others." And then stage three. Hopefully you'll say, "Well, if they're doing it at Florida State and Texas A&M, then I'll try it." And then, ultimately, we're going to get you to stage four where you're going to say, "I can't believe I did it any other way." That's the level you want to get to. Move from "This ain't for me" to "It's OK for others" to "I'll try it" to "I can't believe I did it any other way." And all of your teammates are going to be in that same continuum. Just make sure you get to "I'll try it" because then I can guarantee you that you'll end up at the stage where "I can't believe I did it any other way."

TRAINED OR UNTRAINED MEMORY

I always thought I had a bad memory. What I have learned is that it's not that you have a bad memory or a good memory. You have a trained memory or an untrained memory. Today, I'm going to train you in a technique that I've used. You have probably seen me use this onstage or, if I've worked with you in person, to teach my audience how to memorize anything. Whether it's going through the ten steps of 4RIP3 or 100 slides in a PowerPoint presentation, you too can memorize anything. The process is exactly the same. So if you can learn how to memorize ten things, you can learn how to memorize 10,000 things.

3 STEPS TO MEMORIZE ANYTHING

Let's get started with understanding how you memorize anything. All you need to know are three things:

1. Location
2. Picture
3. Meaning

I'm going give you a location. Then we're going to create a picture and we're going to put that picture on the location I gave you. And then we're going to give that picture meaning. And through that process, you're going to memorize the 4RIP3 System here in about 20 minutes.

So stand up, please, listening to this audio. Yes, actually stand up. Get out of your chair. Get off your seats and your feet and join me in memorizing 4RIP3. Just stand up, and let's get started.

THE 10 LOCATIONS OF SKELETON FILES

Take your hand, and put your right hand on top of your head. The reason we use our right hand is that we'll use our left hand for something later that you want to memorize.

Location one is the top of your head. So take your right hand and touch yourself on the top of your head. And I want you say with me: *Location one is my head. Location one is my head. Location one is my head.*

Now go ahead and touch your nose. *Location two is my nose. Location two is my nose.*

Location three is my mouth. Location three is my mouth.

Location four is my ribs. Location four is my ribs.

And location five is my abs. Location five is my abs.

So let's review. Location one is your head. Location two is your nose. Location three is your mouth. Location four is your ribs. Location five is your abs.

Well, here we go. Let's continue. *Number six is your hips. Number six is your hips. Number six is your hips.*

Number seven is your knees. Number seven is your knees.

Number eight is your shins. Number eight is your shins.

Number nine is your feet. Number nine is your feet.

And number ten is the ground. Number ten is the ground.

What's number six? Hips. What's number seven? Knees. What's number eight? Shins. What's number nine? Feet. And what's number ten? Ground.

Let's review. Number one is your head. Two is your nose. Three is your mouth. Four is your ribs. Five is your abs. Six is your hips. Seven is your knees. Eight is your shins. Nine is your feet. And ten is the ground.

PAINTING PICTURES ON THE LOCATIONS

LOCATION 1 – COMPETE IN THE PRESENT

Well, now that you've memorized the ten locations, let's start to embed the pictures into those locations. I want you to take your hand and put it on top of your head; then imagine, either with your eyes closed or your eyes open, that you can see and feel, on top of your head, a giant present.

Like a Christmas present or a birthday present. As you look inside of that present, you see everything that you own – all of your belongings. You are living inside of that present, and as you look at yourself living inside of that present, you're taking deep breaths. Imagine if you saw that. You'd never forget it. And you're probably thinking, "Wow - this is crazy. This is crazy."

But what you just learned was the number one thing that mentally tough athletes do, and the most important part of the 4RIP3 System is to live in the present. And how do you live in the present? You take a deep breath. So you live in the present by taking a deep breath.

CHECK FOR UNDERSTANDING

Now do you understand what you just did? Location one is the head. The picture is the present with all of your belongings, living in the present, and you're taking a deep breath. The meaning is this: To live in the present moment and compete in the present moment, you get there by taking a deep breath. And that's priority number one.

LOCATION 2 – STICK TO THE PROCESS

What's number two? In your nose, see a staircase because we're going to go step by step. There's a staircase with a pro athlete. So pick any pro athlete. I'm going to take Jennie Finch. And Jennie Finch is running up that staircase, up my nose. And she's got a softball. And she's going one step at a time, and she's bouncing the softball on every step.

I don't know which pro athlete you're thinking of, but see that athlete running up your nose, bouncing a softball on every step because in softball we play one pitch at a time. The softball represents one pitch at a time.

If you're in college or high school, you go through the season and graduate from school one step at a time. We have to take care of today before we take care of tomorrow; today is the most important step. So the steps represent one step at a time and the softball represents one pitch at a time.

Why the pro athlete? Because this is the pro-cess. Or as we say, process. So what's the second thing we do? We focus on the process. We go through school and life one step at a time. We play softball one pitch at a time.

REVIEW

What was number one? Number one was: Live in the present by taking a deep breath. Number two was: Go through school and life one step at a time. Play softball one pitch at a time. That's called focusing on the process.

LOCATION 3 – CONTROL WHAT YOU CAN

Let's go to number three. Inside of your mouth, imagine your tongue just magically transformed into a remote control. Your tongue is a remote control. If you stuck your tongue out and you saw a remote control, you'd never forget it. And that remote control is actually shaped and looks like an ape. It looks like an ape, and it's a hairy remote control. And the remote control has two little arms, beating itself on the chest, going "ahhhhh" like King Kong. An ape.

A remote control that's an ape. Why is that significant? What's the meaning? Because you have to control what you can control. Acronyms are a great way to memorize anything and the acronym for what you can control is APE: Attitude and Appearance (your body language); Perspective and Process (how you see things and how you prepare); and then your Effort, your Energy and your Emotions. APE - a simple way to help you remember what you can control.

REVIEW

So let's review. What was number three? Control what you can control, which is your APE. What's number two? Go one step at a time, play one pitch at a time, called the process. What was number one? Live in the present moment and get there by taking a deep breath.

LOCATION 4 – BE POSITIVE

Now, let's go down to number four. Number four is your ribs. I want you to imagine you just got out of the shower, you're toweling off and you see a tattoo on your ribs. And it's a plus sign.

In math, what does plus mean? Plus means be positive. As a softball player – remembering this is a game of failure – we've got to be positive. But what does it actually mean to be positive? You see, a lot of coaches and athletes I work with in softball think that being positive means you're OK with failure. It's OK to not win. That's not my perspective of being positive.

Being positive really comes down to three things:

1. Turn *have to* into *want to*.
2. Know that you haven't done it YET.
3. No matter how difficult it gets, remember: Difficult compared to what.

TURN HAVE TO INTO WANT TO

So being positive means turning have to into want to. I don't have to work out. I want to. I don't have to get up early and hit off a tee in my garage. I want to. I don't have to go to the weight room. I want to. I don't have to make sound nutritional decisions and decisions around how I invest my social time. I want to.

I CAN'T DO IT YET

If I can't throw 70, I can't do it yet. If I can't hit the ball out of the park, I can't do it yet. If I haven't learned how to be a great slap hitter, I haven't done it yet. Haven't done what? Yet.

COMPARED TO WHAT

No matter how difficult your situation gets, always remember the three magic words: Compared to what. No matter how bad your situation is, there's always someone who's had it much worse and has come out on top. And so can you.

Remember, anything that anyone else can do, you can do. You just haven't done it yet. And you have to remember that "compared to what" others have overcome, so can you.

In my book, *The Mental Conditioning Manual*, we talk about the perspective poster. And the perspective poster is a collage of images, so that when you look at it the poster reminds you of very important aspects of being positive. It reminds you to keep a "compared to what" mentality and to have the attitude of gratitude.

I would encourage you to keep an attitude of gratitude journal on your iPhone or in a journal somewhere. And once a day write down one thing that you're grateful for, because gratitude is like a muscle. Every time you write down something you're grateful for, you strengthen that muscle, and gratitude and happiness travel together.

GRATITUDE AND HAPPINESS

I've never met someone who has a high level of gratitude and low level of happiness. It just doesn't work. If you have gratitude, you have happiness. And when you have high gratitude and high happiness, you have a highly positive mentality. What that means is that you can withstand adversity, and this game of softball is going to knock you to the canvas. You better be able to handle the adversity built into the game of softball or you're just not going to be a good player.

And the best part of adversity is that it is a part of life. There will always be adversity in life.

WINNERS AND LEARNERS

One of the greatest perspectives you can take in being positive is that there are winners and learners. Don't say winners and losers. The only time you're a loser is when you stop learning. You see, you may lose a game, but you may learn a lesson that makes you a better player.

There's nothing bad about losing. If you win every game, you're not playing in the right league. If you lose all the time, that means you're going to get better. Be a winner and, most importantly, be a learner. Know the only time you're a loser is when you stop learning.

Let's review being positive. Turn have-to's into want-to's. You haven't done it yet and compared to what. Have that attitude of gratitude and be a learner.

REVIEW

Let's review. Number one: Live in the present. Get there by taking a deep breath. Number two: Focus on the process. Go through school and life one step at a time. Play softball one pitch at a time. Inside of your mouth, your tongue has turned into a remote control shaped as an ape. What does that mean? Control what you can control. What is it you control? Your APE – Attitude and Appearance, Process and Perspective, and your Efforts, Energy and Emotion. And number four: That's right, be positive.

LOCATION 5 – MENTAL IMAGERY

Now let's go to number five. On your abs is an iPad showing a highlight video of you playing your best softball, the best softball you've ever played. Right now, look at your abs, feel your abs and see that highlight video. You're just crushing the ball all over the yard, making great plays with the glove and pounding that strike zone – just dominant in the circle. That's mental imagery you are doing.

Every time you see yourself playing well, you're recruiting that psycho-neuromuscular pathway. What does that mean? In English, that's the blueprint from your brain to your body that says, "This is how I want to play." So when you do mental imagery, it helps with confidence. When you do mental imagery, it builds up that preparation inside of you to play at a higher level because the brain doesn't recognize what you physically do and what you mentally image as being different. It recognizes them as the same. So you're recruiting the same psycho-neuromuscular pathway to be able to execute that skill by visualizing.

PILLOW AND POTTY TRAINING

The softball players I work with do mental imagery every night. When the head hits the pillow – you're going to take five at-bats.

Head hits the pillow – you're going to strike out five hitters, you're going to make five great plays, defensively. For some of the college teams I work with, we call it potty training. Every time you go to the bathroom, you sit down and you do mental imagery. You're going to be in there anyway. You might as well make yourself a better player. Visualize yourself playing at your best.

REVIEW

So let's review. Number one: Live in the present by taking a deep breath. Number two: Focus on the process. Number three: Control what you can control. Four: Be positive. Five: Use mental imagery.

LOCATION 6 - ROUTINES

Our numbers one through five Skeleton files were above your belt. And numbers six through ten are below your belt. So number six is your hips. Number six is your hips, and for the image on your hips I want you to see an hourglass. And when you see an hourglass, I want you to think about a routine. Now why is an hourglass like a routine? Well, if you put your hands out in front of you about shoulder width, and then you bring your hands together by about your belly button, and then you make a straight line down and then bring your hands out, it's like an hourglass shape. Go ahead and do that.

As you see that hourglass shape, that's what happens in softball. The pitcher gets ready to throw. You step in the ready position, defensively. You play that pitch, you come out, you walk up to home plate, you get in the batter's box, you play that pitch, you step out and get the sign from third, you step back in the box, you play that pitch, you step out and get the sign from third, you step back in the box, you play that pitch. So there's a rhythm and a routine to softball.

When we talk more about routines, you'll understand that routines are the foundation of consistency. And softball is a game of consistency, especially when you're talking about playing at that elite level. When you're talking about trying to win a conference championship, or a regional/super regional/national championship, it's all about consistency and execution of the routine because the routine is the process that keeps you in the present moment.

The routine helps you to stay positive. And we always do mental imagery as a part of our pre-pitch routine. We have pre-pitch routines. We have pre-game routines. We've got morning routines, night routines to help us be a machine of consistency as an elite-level, one-pitch warrior in the game of softball. So number six is about having routines.

Now take your hip. Take your hand and go to your hip. And as you hit yourself on the hip say, "Routines." Say what? Routines.

REVIEW

Now, put your hand back on your head. Number one review: Live in the present. Number two: Touch your nose. Focus on the process. Number three: As you're touching your mouth, control what you can control. Number four: Touch those ribs. Be what? Positive. Number five: Use mental imagery as you're rubbing your abs. And number six, as you're hitting your hip, is about having a routine.

LOCATION 7 – RECOGNIZE YOUR SIGNALS

Now if you go down to your knees, put your hands behind your knees. And I want you to feel, behind your knees, that there's a car wreck.

We're talking about the letters "R" now. There's a wreck behind you for "recognize." So the car wreck, underneath signal lights on your knees, is the picture that I want you to recognize for your signal lights. As we get into the "R" of recognizing, we're going to talk about recognizing when you're in green and when you're in red. When you're in green, you play the next pitch. When you're in red, you have to stop and slow yourself down.

LOCATION 8 – RELEASE / FLUSH IT

Now if you go to your shins, tattooed down your right shin is the word "release." So imagine some Old English script tattoo.

Donald "Cowboy" Cerrone is one of my favorite MMA fighters, and he has the words "Play Time" tattooed on his shin because he likes to play violent games with his shins and kick people. Well, we don't want to do that, but we want to see the same sort of lettering that says "release" down our shin. "Release."

And our left shin is a toilet. Remember that you can picture anything - and right now imagine your left shin is a toilet. So you've got the word "release" in red written down your right leg, and on the left shin is the picture of a toilet. What does that mean? When we're in red lights, we want to release or flush it. Red lights - we release or flush it.

LOCATION 9 – REFOCUS ON THE NEXT PITCH

Now if you look down at your feet, they are green. When you go back to your knees and recognize red, you release or flush it. When you recognize green, you skip your shins and go to your feet. If you look at your left foot, there's a camera lens there and we're going to refocus that camera lens.

We refocus on the left foot and when we go to the right foot, we find softball stitching – another tattoo that says "next pitch." And it actually comes out of your foot like a ball. It's like a huge growth and a softball coming out of your foot. You'd never forget it if you saw it. And it says "next pitch."

So what do we do when we recognize green lights? We refocus on the next pitch. We are in green lights and so we refocus on the next pitch.

LOCATION 10 – DOMINATE THE DAY

If you look down at the ground, your number ten file is a Domino's Pizza box. And there's a huge, cheesy, juicy, saucy pizza in there. You're going to take your foot and you're going to step on that Domino's Pizza box, and the sauce and cheese are going to go flying everywhere. And you're going to yell, "Dominate the day!"

Stepping on the Domino's Pizza box is the picture. And the meaning is: Dominate the day.

REVIEW

So what are the ten steps to becoming a master of the mental game with the 4RIP3 System and dominating the day in softball? Well, let's review.

Number one is you touch the top of your head as you live in the present.

Number two: You focus on the process.

Number three: Inside of your mouth, you control what you can control.

Number four: Be positive.

Number five: Use mental imagery.

Number six: Have a thing called a routine.

Number seven: On your knees, recognize your signal lights.

Number eight: If it's red, you flush it and release.

Number nine: If it's green, you refocus on the next pitch.

Number ten: And that's how you dominate the day.

CONGRATULATIONS

Wow! You just memorized the ten steps of mental toughness. What took me two years of graduate school to learn, you just learned in 20 minutes.

Now, as we go through these next eight audios, we're going to dig deep into how to apply all of these aspects of the 4RIP3 System specifically to your softball performance.

What you must, absolutely must, do is review this 4RIP3 System using your skeleton files, your locations, your pictures and the meanings that you gave those pictures – in front of your team, with your teammates, in front of your mirror – so that you know it.

And coaches, if you're listening to this with your team, you want to have a player, every day, stand before the team and do exactly this: Stand there as if the rest of teammates are at a youth softball camp and that player is the greatest player in the history of the game, and talk about mental toughness. It would go like this:

REVIEW AT PRACTICE EACH DAY WITH TEAM

So there are ten steps to mental toughness in our 4RIP3 System. The first thing we do is live in the present moment, and we get there by taking deep breaths. That helps us to play one pitch at a time, which is a part of our process. You see, we go through the game, every day, step by step. We go through class step by step, one step at a time. And we play softball one pitch at a time, always focusing on the things we can control.

And a simple way to remember what you can control is the acronym APE: Attitude and Appearance (appearance is your body language). Perspective (how you see things in your preparation) and your Process (how you get ready to play). And then your Effort, your Energy and your Emotions. We also stay positive. It's a key part. What does that mean? It means turn have-to's into want-to's, know that you haven't done it yet, and have a "compared to what" mentality and an attitude of gratitude.

We also use mental imagery and visualize ourselves playing well because the brain does not know the difference between what you visualize and what you really do. It's processed the same way.

We have routines to keep us consistent. And inside of those routines, we recognize our signal lights. And if we recognize a red light, we flush it or release. If we recognize a green light, we refocus on the next pitch. And that's how we absolutely, positively dominate the day.

Great show making time for your mental conditioning today, using 4RIP3 as your mission and knowing that you can memorize anything - because you're not born with a great memory but are trained to have a great memory. You are training yourself to be an elite, one-pitch warrior who will dominate on the diamond. Looking forward to our next audio. Make sure you practice this skeleton file system.

Making 4RIP3 Your Mission and Memorizing Anything

REVIEW SHEET

1. Four Stages of Commitment:
    - (1) J
    - (2) W
    - (3) C
    - (4) M
2. Four Stages of Acceptance:
    - (1) This Ain't
    - (2) Ok for
    - (3) I'll
    - (4) I Can't
3. Three Steps to Memorizing Anything
    - (1) L
    - (2) P
    - (3) M
4. The Right-hand Skeleton Files
    - Location
    - Picture
    - Meaning

1) Head
   - You living inside a present & breathing
   - Live in the present moment by breathing

2) Nose
   - Staircase, PRO athlete, one step/ball
   - Stick with the process of one step/pitch at a time

3) Mouth
   - Remote control shaped as an ape
   - Control what you can control

4) Ribs
   - Plus sign with words in, above and below
   - Positive, have to-want to, yet, compared to what

5) Abs
	A highlight video of you playing softball
	Use mental imagery
6) Hips
	Hourglass
	Routines
7) Knees
	Car wreck under signal lights
	Recognize your signal lights
8) Shins
	Tattooed in RED; it says RELEASE / Toilet
	Release the last pitch - flush it
9) Feet
	Camera on left foot to refocus; right = next pitch
	Get green and refocus on the next pitch
10) Ground
	Domino's Pizza box that you smash
	Dominate the Day

COMPETE IN THE PRESENT MOMENT ONE PITCH AT A TIME

Well, how are you doing with your skeleton file system and memorization of 4RIP3? Today we're going to cover how you get yourself to live more and compete more in the present moment, one pitch at a time.

SKELETON FILE SYSTEM REVIEW

Before we dive into the present moment and playing one pitch at a time, let's review your 4RIP3 skeleton file system.

So with your skeleton file, stand up. Remember what was on top of your head?

That was the present.

What was in your nose?

That was the process.

What was in your mouth?

Control what you can control, a key part of the process.

What was on your ribs?

To stay positive, to turn those have-to's into want-to's; to know "I haven't done it yet"; and to think "Compared to what."

What was on your abs?

Mental imagery.

Your hips were about routines.

Your knees were to recognize your signal lights.

Your shins were to release and flush it.

Your feet were to refocus on the next pitch.

That's how you dominate the day!!!!

How are you doing at dominating the day? Have you gotten the skeleton file system locked down? I bet you have. If you've made it this far, into day three, I'm impressed with your commitment to being a master of the mental game.

We're going to pick up the pace and go a little bit faster in these next chapters because now you know the system.

Let's talk about applying the system.

You see, the application of the system, the whole goal of the 4RIP3 System, is that you compete one pitch at a time. The last pitch is history. Future pitches – those are a mystery. Today, with this pitch, is a gift. That's why we call it the present.

EACH PITCH HAS A LIFE AND HISTORY

Treat that gift, treat this pitch, this one pitch, as if it has a life and history of its own. Treat this pitch as if that were the game. In softball, every game's going to come down to probably three or four pitches that are going to make the difference. You never know when those pitches are going to come, so you have to play them all as if they're going to be the one that makes the difference.

COMPETE IN THE PRESENT MOMENT

And how do you compete on each pitch as if it's going to be the one that makes the difference? Well, you live in the present moment.

The most important day of your softball career is today. *Today* is the most important day of your career. Not the national championship. Not your signing day. It's today, because that's all you can control. Yesterday is history. Tomorrow's a mystery. Today is a gift. That's why we call it the present.

So, whether you're talking about the days of your career or the pitches of the game, it's all about going one at a time. Don't count the days as an elite-level softball player. Make the days count.

Again, don't count the days. Make the days count.

Remember that today plus today plus today equals your season and your career.

The time is now and the place is here.

SPEND vs. INVEST TIME

Do you know the difference between spending and investing?

Elite-level softball players don't spend time. They invest time. People who fall short of their goal, people that count the days – they spend time. You invest time. That's what separates you from the other people on the planet that are competing for what you want. You invest, and you grow. They spend, and they stay the same.

If you had that bank account that gave you $86,400 every single day, and when you woke up it gave you another $86,400 regardless of how much you spent or how much you invested, what would you do with that account? You'd drain it, wouldn't you? You'd make investments to try to grow it to help generations of your family to come. You might give it to your friends. You might help people who are in need. But you'd invest all of that $86,400 somewhere and into something. Well, you have that bank account. It's called "time to play the game of softball."

INVEST YOUR $86,400

Every day when you wake up, you get 86,400 seconds to invest into your softball career to make you the absolute best that you can be. And when you wake up every morning, remember you are a woman who is on a mission. You have to be clear in your mission. And if we were working together, the questions I would ask you every day or the questions I would have you answer by text message would be: What are you working on today in training or at practice? What is your mission? What are you working on today to help you create the vision of the future that you want?

HOW DO YOU DEFINE SUCCESS?

There are many different definitions of success. It might be winning games, it might be financial, it might be family.

I heard someone once say, "The definition of success is constantly moving towards the vision of your best future."

"Well," I thought, "That's pretty good. The definition of success is constantly taking steps towards the vision of your best future."

Then the question becomes: How big is the vision of your future? You may know people who are very, very happy. And you look at their life and you think, "Wow - Why don't they have a bigger vision for their future?" Well, it's their life. Ask them.

You see, sometimes I think, as softball players and as young women in general, we get frustrated because maybe other people don't have the same vision that we do. But you need to focus on YOUR vision. You need to focus on what you're trying to do and not get frustrated because other people don't share your vision.

Success is taking those steps toward creating the best vision of your future. And you do that on a daily basis. You do that day to day, pitch to pitch, moment to moment. And it starts by having pre-practice goals and a mission for your day to get you in the present moment.

HOW TO GET IN THE PRESENT

One way you can get yourself into the present at practice and for training is to write down in your cell phone your mission for that day.

You can also take a dry erase marker and write it on the mirror in your bedroom. You can write it down on index cards, stick them in your pocket and carry them with you so you have your goals with you every single day.

Now, there are three exercises that I'm going to train you on for how to do that. I want you to do at least one of them every day, to train yourself to stay in the present moment. This may be the most critical piece of the whole puzzle.

THREE MAJOR EXERCISES

There are three major exercises that we do on a routine basis. And if I'm working with your high school or college program, we're going to build these into a part of practice so that we do them daily.

Number one is concentration grids.

Number two is the 5-4-3-2-1 relaxation and focus exercise.

Number three is the inhale and exhale for 6 to 8, 8 to 10 exercise.

And what these exercises are doing is training you to stay in the present moment as you take deep breaths. When you're in the game of softball and you take a deep breath in the circle, defensively, on the bases or at the plate, that's going to pull you back to that present moment. And that's the gateway for you playing one pitch at a time.

THE BREATH IN SOFTBALL

So before you step into your defensive circle or your defensive routine, you're going to take a breath. Before you throw that pitch, you're going to take a breath. Before you step in the box, you're going to take a breath. And as you're on first base or whatever base you're on, before you get into your lead, you're going to take that deep breath. Before you get ready to take that rocket start lead and explode off that base, you take that breath, you sink in and you're ready go to.

That's how we build the breath into those essential parts of softball so that we stay in the present moment. If you want to take a deep breath with the bases loaded, 3-2 count, and have yourself slow down and get in the present moment, you've got to train that breath off the field.

CONCENTRATION GRIDS

39	48	59	28	71	26	34	70	95	06
21	91	42	12	30	84	76	97	61	75
58	08	85	32	45	66	36	63	23	29
96	80	00	88	89	11	25	57	02	90
74	33	56	93	52	73	04	10	49	19
87	09	16	81	69	38	64	50	83	41
31	01	40	47	18	77	24	14	13	60
79	72	05	51	82	55	15	17	44	94
54	35	53	68	65	20	03	99	86	27
67	46	07	78	22	92	37	62	98	43

So, here's how it works with concentration grids. You train yourself to focus for a longer period of time, and you train yourself to recognize when your mind wanders out of the present moment.

You're going to have a grid that has 100 numbers on it, 00-99. And there are infinite ways to do it. My recommendation is that you start with the grid face down, turn it over and go for three minutes. And as you go for three minutes, see how many numbers you can cross off. Cross the numbers off completely so you don't look at them again. And then after three minutes, write down the time that you have because measurement equals motivation. The reason why we keep track of concentration grid times is because measurement equals motivation, and if we see progress, motivation isn't a problem - so keep track of your times and measure your progress over time.

You can also work the grid by going 00-99 and see how long it takes you. You can go for shorter periods of time, 30 seconds at a time. You can go for odd numbers, even numbers. You can go backwards.

You can do it with music playing or people trying to distract you by screaming at you at as you go through and try to get to ten numbers as quick as possible. There are many different ways you can do it; be creative. The key with concentration grids is to go one number at a time, just like you want to go one pitch at a time. And when your mind wanders, bring it back to the next number, just like you are going to bring it back to the next pitch.

I encourage you to work with the concentration grids in the back of this book and then build them into your routine. If you're a coach or listening to this and you facilitate a practice, take a concentration grid, get it laminated, get a dry erase marker and a clipboard. Have your players sit down as they come out of the batting cage, and as the hitter is waiting to get back in and take her round of swings again, have her sit down and work a concentration grid.

5-4-3-2-1 BREATHING EXERCISE

Another way you can train on your present-moment focus is to sit down and focus on your breathing with the 5-4-3-2-1 audio exercise in this program.

I'm also going to extract from audio 03 and make a separate track that we'll call track 03A; it will have just this exercise should you want to get to it easier. We will also have a track called 03B, which will be the inhale/exhale exercise.

So with the 5-4-3-2-1, this will train you to keep your mind in the moment. We're doing a simple body scan. And you're going to keep your mind in the body part that we mentioned. So when I say "five," put your awareness in your toes, the balls of your feet, your arches, etc. You are to keep your mind in that part of your body.

As we progress through the body, keep your mind in that body part. Keep your focus there, and focus on your breathing.

So let's begin.

5-4-3-2-1 BREATHING EXERCISE SCRIPT

This is the 5-4-3-2-1 relaxation and focus exercise. Please sit up straight in your chair, feet flat on the floor, hands on your lap. Fix your eyes on a spot on the wall in front of you and focus on that spot. Focus on that spot, and now let your eyes gently shut. As you inhale, breathe nice and deep through your nose, then exhale out your mouth.

In through your nose, out through your mouth – one breath at a time. Become present with your breath. Everything else fades away. As we play softball, we want to go one pitch at a time. As we focus on our breath here, we want to go one breath at a time.

So as you continue to focus on your breathing, when you hear the number five, put your awareness into your toes, the balls of your feet, your arches, your ankles, your Achilles, your calves, your shins as they release, relax and let go.

And when you hear the number four, focus on your quads, your knees, your hamstrings, your hips – your whole lower body. Now just release, relax and let go.

And when you hear the number three, focus on your lower back, your mid-back, your upper back, your abs, your obliques, your ribs – your whole torso. Now just release, relax and let go.

And when you hear the number two, concentrate on your traps, your shoulders, your biceps, your triceps, your elbows, your forearms, your hands, your fingers. Release, relax and let go.

And when you hear the number one, focus on the back of your neck, the back of your head, your forehead, your eyes, your cheeks, your jaw. Your lips gently part, and the tongue just hangs in your mouth as complete and total body relaxation and focus take over. And you realize that the more relaxed you become, the better you might feel. And the better you might feel, the more relaxed you might want to become.

Please take one more good, deep breath and exhale, as that concludes your 5-4-3-2-1 breathing and focus exercise.

REFLECTION ON EXERCISE

Well, how'd you do? Did you find your heart rate slowing down and did you feel a little more quiet-minded, a little more relaxed? Now you probably are in such a relaxed state you may be thinking, "This is great, but I don't want to play softball like this - I've got to be a little bit more amped up." And yes, you do. But you also must understand that you have to be in control of yourself before you can control your performance.

In the game of softball, you must be in control of yourself before you can control your performance. And self-control comes from the deep breath. So that's why we condition ourselves to be in the moment. We condition ourselves to stay in control of ourselves, and we do that through breathing.

So if you can use this breathing exercise on your own, you increase your chances of having the ability to relax and gain control of yourself as a weapon in your arsenal as a one-pitch warrior, the ability to slow yourself down and stay in the present.

INHALE & EXHALE EXERCISE

Now, let's take you through the second exercise. This is an inhale/exhale exercise where you're going to count 6 to 8 on the inhale and 8 to 10 on the exhale. You're going to imagine a number flashing in your field of vision. It's like a number on a screen.

If you've been to one of my live seminars, you have seen this visual where the number is flying at you. And that's all you're doing as I say, "Two, three, four, five." You're just seeing that number in your field of vision.

INHALE & EXHALE EXERCISE SCRIPT

Let's begin. Would you please sit up straight with your feet flat on the floor, hands on the lap in front of you as we begin our inhale/exhale, 6 to 8 and 8 to 10, exercise.

As you gently close your eyes and begin to focus on your breathing in this exercise, your goal is to keep your mind on the number as it flashes in your field of vision. We will take five breaths. You may progress, over time, to do this on your own without the audio and work to try to get to ten breaths. Every time you recognize your mind is wandering, just bring it back to that next number in that current breath.

We will begin with inhale in five, four, three, two, one.

Inhale, two, three, four, five, six, seven, eight. Exhale, two, three, four, five, six, seven, eight, nine, ten.

Inhale, two, three, four, five, six, seven, eight. Exhale, two, three, four, five, six, seven, eight, nine, ten.

Inhale, two, three, four, five, six, seven, eight. Exhale, two, three, four, five, six, seven, eight, nine, ten.

Inhale, two, three, four, five, six, seven, eight. Exhale, two, three, four, five, six, seven, eight, nine, ten.

Inhale, two, three, four, five, six, seven, eight. Exhale, two, three, four, five, six, seven, eight, nine, ten.

Please take one more good, deep breath and open your eyes, as this concludes your inhale/exhale exercise.

INHALE & EXHALE EXERCISE REFLECTION

Well, how'd you do? Did you recognize when your mind wandered off that number you were supposed to have in your field of vision? Were you able to pull it back to the next number? Many of you probably had, as you inhaled, a full breath as I was saying, "three, four, five." And you were sitting there trying to hold your breath. You'll find, over time, that in doing that exercise, just like anything else, your breath will smooth in transition with the number.

So there you have it. Three ways you can train your present-moment focus.

1. Concentration grids

2. The 5-4-3-2-1 exercise

3. The inhale/exhale exercise

All of these are available on the CD portion of this program, and if you go to briancain.com/softball, you'll be able to download as many concentration grids as you want and also get these two audios.

Also, use that tactic of writing down your goals on your mirror with a dry erase marker, on a card that you carry with you, or somewhere so you have it with you every single day.

Again, know that one of the best learning strategies is to do a little a lot – not a lot a little - and this applies to your breathing and focus training.

If you're a coach listening to this, take your team through this exercise by playing the audio for them, or you yourself can take the team through this on your own for two minutes before practice.

Know that when you train that relaxation response and you learn to slow yourself down and be in control of yourself, your performance will dramatically improve.

The most important thing here is to know that you must be in control of yourself before you can control your performance.

Thanks for making time today to DOMINATE this audio and chapter. Remember, if you want more, you must become more - and you are becoming more by listening to these audios and reading this book.

Compete in the Present Moment One Pitch at a Time

REVIEW SHEET

Cain's 4_ _ _ 3 System for Training Mental Toughness in Softball

R1 = R_____   I = M_____

R2 = R_____   P1 = P_____

R3 = R_____   P2 = P_____

R4 = R_____   P3 = P_____

1. The goal of the 4RIP3 System is that you compete _____ pitch at a time.

2. When is the most important day of your softball career? T_____ is the most important day.

3. Don't count the days... _____.

4. Today + Today + T_____ = Your S_____ and your _____.

5. The time is _____ and the place is _____.

6. Your bank account credits you with how much money every morning? $_____

7. The question I will ask you the most when I show up at practice is _____?

8. Setting pre-practice goals helps you to get into the _____ _____.

9. There are three major exercises that we do on a routine basis that help you to train your present-moment focus:

    (1) C_____ grids

    (2) _____ Relaxation and focus exercise

    (3) _____ 6-8 / 8-10 exercise

10. By using the _____ you can train yourself to focus for a longer period of time and recognize when your mind wanders out of the present moment.

11. Be sure to keep track of your concentration grid times because _____.

12. One of the best learning strategies is to do a little a lot, _____, and this applies to breathing.

13. You are training your relaxation response when you do breathing exercises. If you want to relax and get present 3-2 bases loaded, you must start training this response off the field.

FOCUS ON THE PROCESS OVER THE OUTCOME

Well, I'm super impressed if you've made it this far, to day four. Did you know that most people never make it a quarter of the way through a personal development program that they invest finances into?

You have made it... Congratulations.

PROCESS OVER OUTCOME APPROACH

And on day four, we're talking about the process over the outcome. You see, the process is all about giving yourself the best chance for success in softball. Everyone wants to talk about winning. That's a mistake because you can't control winning. What you can control is how you play. And if you play your best, you give yourself the best chance for success. And that's what the process and this audio are all about. We want to identify the key factors that, if you focus on them, will give you the best chance for success.

4RIP3 REVIEW

Now let's do a quick review of our 4RIP3 System. With your right-hand skeleton files, you should have this down now like your birthday. I want you to run through it with me.

So right hand on top of head. Live in the –

Your nose. Focus on the –

And your mouth. Control what you –

On your ribs. Be what? That means compared to – Haven't done it -? Turn have-to into –.

Number five is use mental –.

Number six is have these things called –.

Number seven, be able to – your –.

Number eight is you go down to your shins and if it's a red light, you flush it or you –.

And number nine, you're going to – on the next pitch.

And number ten, obviously, you're going to (my favorite) dominate the day.

CONTROL WHAT YOU CAN CONTROL

Now, part of dominating the day is that process of controlling what you can control and, again, knowing that your goal must be in your control. You see, the process is really about two things: Identifying the steps you must take to get to where you want to be and controlling what you can control. So imagine a staircase. At the top of that staircase are the goals, dreams and things that you want to accomplish and get out of your life.

THE STAIRCASE TO YOUR GOALS

The staircase is the process, the steps you have to take to get to where you want to be – one of the best visuals I've ever seen.

So, you start by putting your goal at the top of that staircase. And then make as many steps as you can to get down to what you need to do today to give yourself the best chance to get to the top of that staircase.

WALK THE STAIRCASE ONE STEP AT A TIME

I used to always go two or three steps at a time to try to get to the top of a staircase as quick as possible, always on a mission. And one of the things that successful people do is to walk 25% faster than the people who are not on a mission. So make sure you also walk faster, 25% faster, than you do right now to help you get to where you want to be, and be on a mission. But also, when you go up that staircase, hit every single step. And the reason why you hit every step is because you cannot skip a step in the process and expect to make it to the top. You've got to hit every single step. So when you go up that staircase, one step at a time, 25% faster, you are reinforcing to yourself the importance of taking just one step at a time.

You see, the process is also about competing with yourself and the game – and never the opponent. Pat Summitt, who was the basketball coach at the University of Tennessee, one of the greatest programs and coaches in the history of college athletics, always said: "We never compete against the other team. We're always competing against a nameless, faceless opponent. We're competing against ourselves to try to play our best."

THE LAW OF AVERAGES

Now there's a thing we talk about in softball called "the law of averages." And the law of averages in the process says that only four things can happen when you play softball:

1. You play well and win.
2. You play well and lose.
3. You play lousy and win.
4. You play lousy and lose.

You see, it's a law. Only one of those four things is going to happen, and what you want to do is play well because you give yourself the best chance to win when you play well. But if you've been around this game for a while, you know that sometimes you play well and you still lose. Sometimes you don't play well at all and you win, and sometimes you play lousy and you lose.

So the goal is to play well, and if you play well, you give yourself the best chance to win.

SEVEN WAYS TO BEAT THE GAME

Now within the process, there are seven ways to beat the game and give yourself the best chance for success. We call these "process-based win indicators." You see, they're part of the process of playing championship softball; if you execute them, you give yourself the best chance for success.

We're going to memorize these seven ways to beat the game by using the location/picture/meaning technique that you've learned with the skeleton files with location, picture and meaning.

This time, we're going to use just your left hand. So if you take your left hand, the left hand is the location. The picture is what you're going to do with your hand. And the meaning is going to be derived from that picture.

NO ERRORS

So here we go. Make a fist like it's number zero. Zero means: Make no errors. What does zero mean? Make no errors.

SCORE FIRST

Put up number one. What does one mean? One means: Score first. What does one mean? Score first.

TWO OUT OF THREE FOR A STRIKE

Put up two fingers. What does two mean? Two means: Execute two out of the first three pitches, to every hitter, for a strike. What's number two? Execute two out of the first three pitches to every hitter for a strike, which means if you run the count to one ball/two strikes instead of two balls/one strike, you have a much greater chance for success – in other words, if the hitter is on or out under three pitches, you have a much better chance for success.

GIVE UP 3 RUNS OR LESS

What's number three mean? Three means: Hold your opponents to three runs or less. When you hold your opponents to three runs or less, you dramatically increase your chances of winning.

54% QUALITY AT-BATS

What's number four? Number four means: Have 54% quality at-bats. You see, for every at-bat, your goal is not to get a hit. The goal is to have a quality at-bat. Remember, the goal must be where? That's right. The goal must be in your control. And you don't control getting hits. You control having quality at-bats. A quality at-bat might be taking a walk, might be getting hit by a pitch, might be moving a runner from second to third with no outs. It's scoring a runner from third base anytime you can. It might be executing a sacrifice bunt, executing a sacrifice fly.

Anything that you do to help your team win could be considered a quality at-bat. Now think about it like this. This is why softball's such a crazy game. Imagine a runner on second and third base, no outs. You hit a ground ball to the second baseman, who throws you out at first, but the runner scores from third and the other runner moves from second to third. Your batting average just went down, but you help your team win. That is what's crazy about softball - your stats can go down but your chance of winning goes up. So the focus is on quality at-bats. That's number four.

SCORE 5 RUNS OR MORE

Number five is: Score five runs or more. If you score five runs or more, you again dramatically increase your chances of winning.

WIN THE FREE BASE – FREEBIE WAR

Now if you take your three fingers and put them in the air – the pointer finger, the middle finger and the ring finger – and make a "W," that's for "freebie war." The freebie war is about getting free bases. It's like turnovers in football. The team that gets more free bases usually wins. Catcher's interference, illegal pitches, walks, hit by a pitch, errors, passed ball – any of those things that give you a free base. If you take free bases, those lead to runs. And runs lead to wins. It's like our process-based staircase. We want to win. What do we have to do to win? Score runs. What do we need to do to score runs? We've got to get free bases. How do we get free bases? We've got to know that winning the freebie war is important and focus on moving up on balls in the dirt, moving runners, et cetera.

SEVEN WAYS TO BEAT GAME REVIEW

So, left hand – seven ways to beat the game. Zero, make no errors. One, score first. Two, execute two out of the three first pitches for a strike. Three, hold opponents to three runs or less. Four, 54% quality at-bats. Five, score five runs or more. "W," win the freebie (free base) war. So you've memorized the 4RIP3 System using your skeleton file system and you've memorized the seven ways to beat the game using your left hand as the location.

KNOW YOUR MISSION

Know that your mission as a hitter – it's real simple - is to have a quality at-bat.

Your mission as a pitcher – real simple: Throw quality pitches.

You see, winning softball games is a by-product of working the process. Winning softball takes care of itself when you have a good process and know your mission and goals for each game, each pitch. Even the way you stand for the National Anthem is a part of your process. How organized you keep your locker or your bag in the dugout and how you manage your time between games is a part of the process for you elite-level, travel softball players.

CONTROL WHAT YOU CAN CONTROL

Now maybe the most important of the process.

I purposely put it at the end of this track so that only you, who are totally committed and are almost halfway through the whole 4RIP3 training program already, would get this because I don't want to give it to people who are not committed. I only want the people that are the most committed, the most elite, to have it.

This is maybe the most important thing you're going to get in this entire program. Suppose that you asked me the following: "Brian, you were a Division I college baseball player. What do you know now that you wish you knew when you were playing that might have made a difference for you?" The thing I know now that I wish I knew then was that you should only focus on things you can control.

So, I want you to make two critical lists: the list of what you can control and the list of what you cannot control. Pause this audio now, and take the time to write down what you can and what you can't control. Pause this audio now.

CAN CONTROL	CANNOT CONTROL
Attitude	Batting Average
Effort	Umpires
	Weather
	Injuries
	Winning
	Other people
	Parents
	Playing time
	Field conditions
	ERA
	Win/loss

personal power

WHAT YOU CAN CONTROL

Thanks for coming back. Now let's talk about the factors that you can control. You see, all you can control in softball is yourself. And remember that image of the remote control that was inside of your mouth? It was APE. All you can control is yourself and your APE: your Attitude, your Appearance (how you carry yourself, your body language) – your Perspective (how you see things, your preparation), your Process – your Effort, your Energy and your Emotions. That's it. Everything else is a waste of time. When you focus on aspects of softball or of life that you can't control, you beat yourself.

WHAT YOU CAN'T CONTROL

Let's identify what you can't control so you don't fall into those traps. You can't control your parents. You can't control your coaches. You can't control umpires, your teammates, opponents, weather, field conditions, playing time, colleges, coaches, scholarships, your ERA, your batting average, bat hops, injuries, fans, media, what softball organizations rank your team and you as a prospect. And you can't control winning.

As a pitcher, you don't control getting outs. You don't even control throwing strikes. How many times have you made a pitch that you knew was a strike and the umpire said "ball" because it's not a strike zone? It's the umpire zone. And because umpires are human beings, they're going to make mistakes. So you cannot allow yourself to let your success come from things outside of your control. Your success must come from the process because if you execute the process, you give yourself the best chance to get those outcomes that you're looking for.

YOU CAN'T CONTROL WINNING

Control what you can control. I hope you're listening, and I hope you are getting this. And maybe you're confused. Which is beautiful.

You may be saying "What you mean, I can't control winning?" You can't. Have you ever played well and lost? Yes. Have you ever played lousy and won? Yes. That's crazy.

You have to focus on playing well and what you can do to give yourself the best chance for success. That is the process. And when you have a good process, you give yourself the best chance for the outcome. You never control the outcome. And you don't have to be in the zone to play your best. I'm not sure the zone exists in softball.

THE ZONE DOES NOT EXIST

For me, the zone is a mixed martial arts match combined with a marathon. It's a grind. The zone is about you going out there and giving yourself the best chance for success, whether you feel like it or not. Act differently than how you feel because how you act is a controllable. How you feel is a non-controllable.

So get rid of feeling and the notion that you have to feel good to play good - get into action and what you must do today. That will be liberating. That will change your life. Stop focusing on how you feel. Start focusing on what you need to do, and go do, because the days that you feel great or the days you feel like garbage, you're going to do about the same.

I've written five books. I write as a part of my morning routine. I write on the days I feel like writing and the days I don't feel like writing. I have learned that the quality of my writing on those days is about the same. Your performance in softball is about the same. Do not beat yourself because you don't feel good. Do not beat yourself because maybe you don't have all the confidence in the world.

CONFIDENCE

Confidence is not a feeling. Confidence is an action. Act big, breathe big, commit big, and go up there as a one-pitch warrior like you're ten feet tall and bulletproof. That's what you can control. You can't control the result. Control your process and give yourself the best chance for success. Identify the steps you need to take, personally and as a program, to get you to where you want to be. Control what you can control. Let go of what you can't, completely, and focus on what you can.

EVEN THE BEST FOCUS IS WRONG AT TIMES

I was just with one of the top college softball programs in the country. Between 2008 and 2011, they won two NCAA national championships. They are one of the best programs in the country, if not the best. They've played in seven of the last eight Women's College World Series. We're talking about the ASU Sun Devils.

And in meeting with the ASU Sun Devils, we said to the team, "Give a percentage to how much you focus on what you can and what you can't control." It was amazing how much they focused on what they could not control. It was similar to most other programs in the country, but these are the elite of the elite.

They were focusing on what they could not control anywhere between 50% to 80% of the time. And they're beating themselves when they're doing it. Now, they're really, really good – seven of the last eight Women's College World Series! If they focused on what they could control as much as they focused on what they couldn't, would they have won more than two? We can never answer that question, but I know what my answer would be.

From this day moving forward, we've got to get them and you to let go of what you can't control and focus only on what you can to give yourself the best chance for success.

Today, let go of what you can't control and be a control freak, freakish about only focusing on what you can control.

Focus on the Process over the Outcome
REVIEW SHEET

1. The process is about giving yourself the best chance _____ _____.

2. The process is about controlling what you _____ _____.

3. Your goal must be in _____.

4. The process is about identifying the _____ you must take to get to where you want to be.

5. The process is about competing with _____ and _____, never the opponent.

6. The law of averages and the process say that four things can happen when you play softball:

    (1) Play well and _____

    (2) Play well and _____

    (3) Play lousy and _____

    (4) Play lousy and _____

7. There are seven ways to beat the game and give yourself the best chance for success. We call these process-based win indicators. They are part of the process of playing championship softball; and if you execute them, you give yourself the best chance for success.

8. We will memorize these using the Location/Picture/Meaning technique on the left hand.

      0 = Make no errors

      1 = Score first

      2 = Execute 2 out of 3 pitches for a strike

      3 = Hold opponent to 3 runs or less

      4 = Have 54% quality at-bats

      5 = Score 5 runs or more

      W = Win the freebie (free base) war

9. Your job as a hitter is to have a _____.

10. Your job as a pitcher is to throw _____.

11. Winning softball games is a _____ of working the process.

12. The way you stand for the National Anthem is a part of the process.

13. How organized your locker is and how you manage your time are parts of the process.

14. You have two critical lists - your lists of what you _____ and _____ control.

STAYING POSITIVE IN A GAME OF FAILURE

Congratulations on making it to day five. Today we're talking about staying positive in a game of failure.

STAY POSITIVE IN A GAME OF FAILURE

Softball is a game of failure, probably the most failure-driven game on the planet. You can do everything right and still not get the result you're looking for.

Imagine that you were playing golf. You stood above the ball and as you executed the swing exactly the way you wanted to, someone ran out on the fairway, caught the ball and laughed at you, and then threw it into a sand trap. Now that would never happen. But that's what happens in softball every day. You step up into the box. You absolutely smoke a pitch, and someone catches it. And then they laugh at you because you're out. But you did everything you possibly could to give yourself the best chance for success.

We're going to keep coming back to that point about the process over the outcome, because process over outcome really is part of having that positive mentality.

WHAT DO POSITIVE PLAYERS DO?

What positive softball players do is turn have-to's into want-to's. They know that there are no have-to's. They focus on making them want-to's. They know that they choose to focus on what they want – not what they're trying to avoid.

You see, positive thinking in softball is focusing on what you want to do – not what you're trying to avoid.

Focusing on having a quality at-bat versus striking out.

Focusing on executing this pitch down in the zone instead of trying not to leave it up.

It's like trying to throw that screwball in for a strike instead of thinking, "OK, don't hit her." You've all been there. You've all said that thing you didn't want to have happen. And then it came true.

NO PINK ELEPHANTS – PICTURES WIN

It's like, right now, don't think about a pink elephant. Immediately, what happens? You start thinking about a pink elephant. Why? Because the brain is a heat-seeking computer that shows you pictures. And you talk to yourself in pictures. So what's the picture you see here? "Don't hit her with a screwball." The brain doesn't recognize the negative of "don't," "can't," or "won't." All it sees is "hit her with a screwball." Or "don't strike out" - the picture you see is "strike out." So the pictures you give to this heat-seeking computer in your head by self-talk are going to put yourself into action to make those images come true.

FOCUS ON WHAT YOU WANT

So you see that positive thinking is focusing on what you want – not what you're trying to avoid.

Positive thinking is knowing that you can do it. You just might not have done it yet.

AMAZING STORY OF BELIEF & BARRIERS

On May 6, 1954, a guy by the name of Roger Bannister was going to go out and run the mile under four minutes. The first person ever to do so. It had never been done.

They said that it was physiologically impossible. Your brain would stop, your lungs would collapse, your heart would die. You can't run that fast. "Your body's not designed to do that" is what everyone said. But Bannister knew different. He was a medical student. And he knew that he could. It just hadn't been done yet.

Bannister knew that there is no success without adversity. Please write that down somewhere. There can be no success without adversity.

And Bannister, at the Olympics just two years before, was a favorite in the one-mile event in Helsinki, and he fell short – didn't medal at all. Out came the critics, out came the negaholics telling Bannister he wasn't good enough. He wasn't fast enough, he wasn't strong enough, he didn't train hard enough.

But that day in Oxford, England - May 6, 1954 - Roger Bannister went out and became the first person ever to run under four minutes. And Roger Bannister changed the landscape of athletics and changed the game of softball forever because by going under four minutes, he proved that there are no physical barriers. The only barriers to overcome are mental barriers, because what happened within one year was that 13 other people broke the four-minute mile barrier, which had never been done before - within one year, 13 people had done it. And now there are high school runners all over the world that are going under four minutes, probably even someone at your school.

The amazing thing is that it took one person to do it and now people all over the world are doing it. Once one person does it and you see that one person do it, you think, "If they can do, I can do it." And that's the same process as what happened with the four-minute mile barrier.

WHY EAT FIRE?

It's the reason why I have people eat fire, bend rebar with their necks and break boards over their heads in my seminars - to prove that if one person can do it, everyone can do it.

So, positive people know: It just hasn't been done yet.

ATTITUDE OF GRATITUDE

Positive people have an attitude of gratitude. They have an attitude of gratitude journal. Here's exactly how I do it. I encourage you to try it this way or a way that's going to work best for you.

On my iPhone, I have an appointment that pops up on my calendar at 8:00 every morning. And the first thing I do is start my day with gratitude, and I write down something that I'm thankful for. Today I wrote down, "I'm thankful for the great softball coaches and players out there that are going to benefit and take their mental game to the next level by using this program."

By writing down one thing you're grateful for every day, you start building that muscle of gratitude. And gratitude and happiness travel together. You can't be grateful and negative at the same time. It just doesn't work that way. So you've got to develop the attitude of gratitude, and you'll be more positive.

COMPARED TO WHAT

You see, positive people also know that other people have it worse. They never make excuses. They use the "compared to what" mentality to give themselves the best peak performance state possible. So how do you create a "compared to what" mentality? You create what we call a perspective poster.

PERSPECTIVE POSTERS

Your perspective poster is a collage of images that remind you of the attitude of gratitude and that compared to what these people have gone though, you too can overcome and be successful. Now I encourage you to make your own personal perspective poster, but then also a team perspective poster. And that team perspective poster must have one personal image from every player or coach on your program that represents something to remind them to have that attitude of gratitude and "compared to what" mentality.

THE VOICE OF SELF-TALK

You see, we've all got this voice inside of our heads. And that voice inside of your head we call "self-talk," or you've heard me refer to it as your red and green assassin. That red and green assassin is either going to tell you what you want to do or tell you what you want to avoid. And the voice inside of your head is either going to tell you that you can or that you can't.

GREEN MEANS GO

The one that tells you that you can is like a green light. Driving a car, when you come to a green light, you go. It's a performance mover. The light that tells you that you can't go is a red light. It's a performance stopper. And you've got to understand and listen to which voice you want to train inside of your head.

TRAIN YOUR WOLF

An old Indian chief had a young baby Indian come up to him and say, "Chief, what do you know now that you wish you knew when you were young?" And the old Indian chief said: "Young son, every Indian has two wolves - one red and one green, and one positive and one negative, and one that helps and one that hurts - that live inside of them. And they fight every single day." And the young boy asked: "Chief, which one wins the battle? Which one's going to win the battle inside of me? The green or the red? The positive or the negative? The good or the bad?" And the old Indian chief said, "Son, the one that's going to win the battle is the one that you train."

So as an elite-level softball player, which voice inside of your head are you training? The one that's positive or the one that's negative? And in my *Mental Conditioning Manual* I give you many examples that you can use to train that positive voice.

iPHONE CONFIDENCE CONDITIONING

So on the iPhone, pull out your calendar, create an appointment that says "confidence conditioning statements."

In the confidence conditioning statements note on your phone write, "I am a one-pitch warrior who controls what I can control."

"I love the challenge and adversity built into softball."

"I am a confident, healthy, energetic athlete who makes my teammates better."

Whatever positive statements or confidence conditioning statements you want to write down, put those in your phone so they pop up every day for you to see. And then you can train your confidence - you train that positive self-talk.

And over time, by doing a little a lot, not a lot a little, that voice inside your head starts to become the one that's positive. So whether you write them down on your mirror or whether you put them inside of your phone, write down some confidence conditioning statements. If you start training yourself to think this way, you'll give yourself the best chance for success.

E + R = O IN SOFTBALL

You see, "E" plus "R" equals "O." Events plus our Response to those events equals the Outcome of what those events will be. Positive people know they can't control events and they can't control outcomes, but they influence the outcomes of those events by choosing their response.

WILL BEATS SKILL

So always, always choose your response positively and know that, regardless of the odds, will beats skill in softball. And the best team never wins. It's always the team that plays the best. So create that confidence resume.

THE CONFIDENCE RESUME

That confidence resume is a list of reasons why you believe in yourself. Good games that you've played, great days of practice that you've had, things that you've learned, coaches you played for or with, great athletes you've been around – write down all the reasons why you should believe in yourself to succeed. We call it a confidence resume. Part of your confidence resume is those confidence conditioning statements that we talked about earlier.

THE BIG ABC'S

And then remember the big ABC's of being positive. ABC: Always Behave Confidently because confidence is a choice. And confidence is an action that's made when you get big. The 2012 University of Alabama softball program had a sign on the door of their locker room and a sign on the door of the bathroom in their dugout that said "Get Big" because the way you carry yourself will significantly influence how you perform.

A lot of people think that their feelings dictate their actions. Change that. Let your actions change your feelings. Act big.

Carry yourself with big body language. Breathe big to keep yourself in the moment and slow the game down, and commit big to what you're about to do. Act big, breathe big, commit big to that pitch, to that moment, to give yourself the best chance for success. Stay positive in this game of failure because the alternative will kill your performance.

4RIP3 Softball Mental Conditioning Program
Staying Positive in a Game of Failure
REVIEW SHEEET

1. Positive thinking is turning your have-to's into _____.

2. Positive thinking is focusing on what you want, not what you _____.

3. Positive thinking is knowing that you can do it - you just might not have done it _____.
(Roger Bannister)

4. Positive people have an attitude of _____ and you can build this by having a gratitude journal.

5. Positive people also know that others have it worse. They never make excuses and use the _____ mentality to give themselves the best peak performance state possible.

6. You should build your attitude of gratitude and positive perspective by creating a perspective _____.

7. The voice inside of your head that either is helping you to succeed or is killing your performance is called the voice of _____.

8. Confidence conditioning statements written down and reviewed on a routine basis will serve as the foundation for creating positive self-talk.

9. E + R = O stands for event plus response = _____. Positive people choose their responses.

10. Positive people know that will beats _____ in softball and the best team never _____.

11. Remember Roger Bannister? What was his significance on softball? There are no physical barriers, just _____ to overcome.

12. Creating a confidence resume is a great way to remind yourself of why you deserve to have success and why you are a good softball player. We all forget our previous wins and successes because we focus so much on what's happening in the future that we forget about our successful past. We must review our past to help us create the future we desire.

13. Get Big and fake it till you make it. Positive people know the BIG ABC's:

    A_____big

    B_____big

    C_____big

MENTAL IMAGERY FOR SOFTBALL PERFORMANCE

Welcome to day six. By now, I know that you have committed the 4RIP3 System to memory.

You know that to live in the present we take a deep breath; focus on the process; go one day, one pitch at a time; control what we can control, which is your APE; stay positive, turn those have-to's into want-to's; know we haven't done it yet; and use the "compared to what" mentality while doing mental imagery. Inside of our routine we are able to recognize, release and then refocus; and we dominate the day.

MENTAL IMAGERY FOR SOFTBALL

Have you ever played rock, paper, scissors? Well, what about roshambo? Most people have played rock, paper, scissors, but they don't think they've played roshambo. If you've played rock, paper, scissors, you've played roshambo - it's just another name for the game. So have you played roshambo? Yes. But until now, you didn't think you had. And have you done mental imagery before? Yes. You just don't know that you had. It's the same principle.

YOU DO IMAGERY WITHOUT KNOWING IT

You see, we're always doing mental imagery. We're always visualizing ourselves, whether it's playing softball, whether it's giving directions to a friend about how to drive to our house. We are always visualizing what it is we want to do. It's the way the brain is wired.

Mental imagery is a skill that will help you to play your best when it means the most. Mental imagery is a skill that will build confidence. And know that mental imagery has also been called visualization and mental rehearsal. And you do this without even knowing you do it.

HIGHLIGHT VIDEOS HELP

Watching highlight videos of yourself or others playing the way you want to play is a great way to help you build the positive mental images that you can refer back to when doing mental imagery. Often, when I'm working with a softball player, I'll sit down with her and we'll watch some quality at-bats that she's had or someone else has had. And after each quality contact or each quality pitch, I have her just close her eyes and imagine herself executing that same pitch, feeling what it would feel like, seeing what it would look like, putting herself in that moment to execute that pitch.

You can do that same thing by jumping onto YouTube and watching highlight videos of other players. If you're a slapper, find some slapper highlighter videos. If you're a left-handed pitcher, find some left-handed pitcher highlight videos and visualize yourself playing that same way.

RELAXATION & USING SENSES HELP

Doing some relaxation before you do imagery is good because when you're in a relaxed state, it sets the stage for more clear and vivid imagery, which goes to work on your subconscious mind, which is driving the whole machine that you are as a softball player.

When you do mental imagery, you want to use as many of your senses as possible – sight, sound, touch, smell, taste. Build in as many senses as you can.

THINKING ABOUT SOFTBALL vs. IMAGERY

Know that doing mental imagery is different than just thinking about playing softball. Now you may be sitting around your house or in the car thinking about playing softball, and that's great. But you want to do solid mental imagery of visualizing yourself playing softball by seeing it, feeling it, hearing it and building those senses in.

As you do mental imagery, the added benefit is you're building what we call mind control, just like when you do those breathing exercises. And mind control leads to body control which leads to skill control. So the better you are at being in control of your mind, the better off you will be at being in control of your body. And then you'll be better off at being in control with executing the skills that are required for you to play championship softball.

WHY IS MENTAL IMAGERY EFFECTIVE?

Mental imagery is effective because the brain processes information, whether you vividly imagine it or physically experience it, with the same psycho-neuromuscular pathways. It's that blueprint for performance. It's why you talk in your sleep and wake up from dreams. The brain processes information, whether you think about it or experience it, as the same.

By visualizing and doing mental imagery, you're creating that psycho-neuromuscular pathway in your body to be able to execute those skills. In English, it's like creating the blueprint for a performance.

FOUR STEPS TO MENTAL IMAGERY

Now there are four steps to effective mental imagery that I'm going to walk you through.

The first is relaxation. We'll get you in a good, relaxed state.

The second is confidence conditioning, where I'll say some confidence conditioning statements like, "I'm a one-pitch warrior who plays with confidence." And I'll have you say that to yourself three times in a relaxed state to start embedding that in your subconscious mind.

Then, we'll go into mental recall. And this is where I need your help. I need you to recall some of your best softball performances. So close your eyes right now. Think about those best softball performances. Where were they? Who were they against? What were you wearing? What were they wearing? What did it look like? What did it sound like? So when I have you recall and go back to these best softball performances, these are the games you're going to remember.

Then we're going to mental rehearsal. And in mental rehearsal, this is going to be setting the stage for your next performance. Now I'm going to talk you through very general mental rehearsal for softball.

COACHES, TAKE NOTICE

And for the coaches listening to this with your teams, if you're going to use this audio, I will say at a specific point, "Coach, if you now want to talk your team through specific aspects of mental imagery for your upcoming performance…" That's when you would talk and just keep your rhythm and the pace and the tempo and the volume of your voice as consistent and monotone as you can to help them to stay in that relaxed state.

I will also create audio 6A, which is just the mental imagery component of this track so you don't have to listen to all of this information about imagery first; you can just get right into it.

PASSIVE vs. ACTIVE IMAGERY

Now softball hitters, you want to do some mental imagery when you're four hitters away. When we start talking about routines, we'll talk about the mental imagery hole. And this is how you build imagery into what we do, actively. You see, the imagery

I'm going to be taking you through in this audio, where you're going to lie down on the ground, is what's called passive mental imagery. And this happens in a relaxed state.

Active mental imagery would be like a pitcher using mental imagery as part of her pre-pitch routine to help her body commit to the pitch she wants to execute or throw.

Hitters are going to use active mental imagery four people away, sitting down on the bench in the dugout, before they go in the hole or on deck to visualize themselves hitting off the pitcher who's throwing.

And again, when you do mental imagery, you want to do a little a lot – not a lot a little – because the more consistent you are with doing mental imagery, the better off you will be and the better, the more significant and longer lasting, the benefits will be.

COACHES, MAKE THIS PART OF THE ROUTINE

Coaches, you can make this 6A mental imagery track a part of your consistent, weekly practice. Athletes, you want to have this track on your iPhone to do mental imagery as a part of your pre-game routine the night before, but also those pre-pitch routines that we do during the games.

MENTAL IMAGERY FOR SOFTBALL SCRIPT

To begin your mental imagery for softball performance training, please either sit up straight in your chair with your feet flat on the floor and your hands in your lap in front of you or, preferably, lie down on the ground or on the floor, flat on your back with your feet flat on the floor as if you're doing a sit-up or legs straight out in front of you.

And as in you're in that good, quiet, comfortable position, please now fix your eyes on a spot on the wall in front of you.

Focus on that spot. And now, let your eyes gently shut. As you inhale, breathe nice and deep through your nose. And exhale, out your mouth.

In through your nose. Out through your mouth. One breath at a time. In through your nose. Out through your mouth. One breath at a time.

PART 1 – RELAXATION TRAINING

As you continue to focus on your breathing, we will begin part one of the four stages of mental imagery with relaxation. And as you continue to focus on your breathing, when you hear the number five, please put your awareness into your toes, the balls of your feet, your arches, your ankles, your Achilles, your calves, your shins.

When you hear the number four: your knees, your quads, your hamstrings, your hips – your whole lower body. Just release, relax and let go.

When you hear the number three: your lower back, your mid-back, your upper back, your abs, your obliques, your ribs – your whole torso. Just release, relax and let go.

And when you hear the number two: your traps, your shoulders, your biceps, your triceps, your elbows, your forearms, your hands, your fingers. Just release, relax and let go.

And when you hear the number one: the back of your neck, the back of your head, your forehead, your eyes, your cheeks, your jaw. Your lips gently part and the tongue just hangs in your mouth as complete and total body relaxation and centering take over. And what you realize is that the more relaxed you become, the better you might feel. And the better you might feel, the more relaxed you might want to become.

As you continue to lie in this quiet, comfortable place, please lift your right leg an inch off the ground and hold it there. Hold it there, hold it there and drop it. And as you drop it, just let the tension go. Just let it go.

And now the other leg, an inch off the ground. Hold it there, hold it there, hold it there. Drop it. Just let that leg go. Just let the ground take the weight.

And now your right arm. Make a fist with your right arm and squeeze it with 25% tension, 50%, 75%, full tension – tight, tight. And release. And just let that arm relax. Just let it go. Just let it go.

Now the left arm, 25% tension, 50%, 75%, full tension – tight, tight, tight. And release. Just let it go. Just let it go and relax.

And now where your head comes in contact with the ground, just push your head back 50%, 50%, 75%, 75%. And relax. And just let your head roll side to side until it finds that good, quiet, comfortable place to call home.

PART 2 – CONFIDENCE CONDITIONING

We will now shift into confidence conditioning. You're to repeat the following phrases to yourself. There's no need to say them out loud. Say each phrase with confidence, with conviction and with belief, with every fiber of your being.

"I play the game one pitch at a time. I play the game one pitch at a time. I play the one pitch at a time.

"I control what I can control and let go of what I can't. I control what I can control and let go of what I can't. I control what I can control and let go of what I can't.

"I am a one-pitch warrior who plays with confidence at all times. I am a one-pitch warrior who plays with confidence at all times. I am a one-pitch warrior who plays with confidence at all times.

"I love the challenge and adversity that is softball. I love the challenge and adversity that is softball. I love the challenge and adversity that is softball."

And now, take another good, deep breath in through your nose, out through your mouth.

PART 3 – MENTAL RECALL

As we move to part three of mental imagery, I want you to recall your best softball performances you've ever had. In your mind, replay those best softball performances as if they're happening now. Hear what each one sounded like. Feel what it felt like. See what it looked like. Make the experience as real as you possibly can. See the colors. Hear the sounds. Smell the smells. Taste the tastes. Make that peak performance as real as you possibly can. See it as if it's happening in HD. Hear it as if it's in stereo sound. Feel it as if it's happening right now, in this moment.

Replay your peak performance softball as if it's happening right now. In this moment, you are the greatest softball player you've ever been. Make this moment as if you are watching a highlight video in your mind of you DOMINATING on the diamond. Now, take a good, deep breath in through your nose, out through your mouth as we move forward to your next softball performance.

PART 4 – MENTAL REHEARSAL

We will now rehearse for your next softball performance. And if your coach or a parent or someone else is there and wants to pause this track and talk you through your next performance, you can do so now. Otherwise, we will continue.

So put yourself in that next softball performance, whether it's practice, a lesson, inner squad game or outside competition. Wherever it is, put yourself on that field where you'll be competing.

Now if you're a pitcher, put yourself in the circle at that field, executing pitches to the best of your ability - always seeing, feeling and hearing the desired outcome. Hitters, put yourself in that batter's box and do the same – see, feel and hear the desired outcome of your performance. Hitters, I want you now to see a pitch away that you're going to drive in the opposite field gap for a double.

Pitchers, I want you to execute a pitch down in the zone that gets a swing and miss.

Pitchers, execute a pitch up in the zone that gets a swing and miss through your rise ball.

Hitters, I want you to take a pitch on the inside part of the plate and drive it down the line into the corner for a double.

And now, play your best softball like a highlight video on repeat, just driving the ball all over the yard, executing pitches – playing your best.

As I count down from ten to zero, speed up those images, feel those images more, make it more real. When we get to zero, take a deep breath and open up your eyes. Ten, nine, eight, seven, six, five, four, three, two, one, zero. Deep breath. Open up your eyes. Bring yourself back to this room, right here, right now as this concludes your mental imagery for softball performance.

CONCLUDING YOUR IMAGERY SESSION

Great show making time for your mental game. By doing mental imagery, you're increasing your ability to perform at the level with which you see in your mind. See positive images and you'll get positive results. Continue to work at your mental game because if you want more, you absolutely, positively must become more. Become more today by working on yourself and at the greatest game in the world – the game of softball.

Mental Imagery for Softball Performance
REVIEW SHEET

1. Mental _____ is also known as visualization and mental rehearsal. You do this without even knowing you do it.

2. Watching _____ videos of yourself or others playing the way you want to play is a great way to help you have positive mental images that you can refer back to when doing your imagery.

3. Doing _____ before you do imagery is a good idea because when you are relaxed, it sets the stage for more clear and vivid images.

4. When doing imagery, you want to use as many of your _____ as possible.

5. Mental imagery is different than _____ about playing softball.

6. M_____ control leads to b_____ control leads to s_____ control.

7. Mental imagery is effective because the brain processes information, whether you vividly imagine it or physically do it, in similar psycho-neuromuscular pathways.

8. There are four steps to effective mental imagery:

    (1) R_____
    (2) C_____
    (3) M_____
    (4) M_____

9. Softball hitters should do some good mental imagery when they are _____ hitters away.

10. Pitchers should do mental imagery as a part of their _____ to help their body commit to the pitch that they want to execute/throw.

11. When doing imagery, you want to do a little a lot, not a lot a little. The more consistent you are, the better off you will be.

12. You should do mental imagery as a part of your pre-game and pre-pitch routine and use the attached audio the night before you compete.

ESTABLISHING ROUTINES FOR CONSISTENT SOFTBALL PERFORMANCE

Welcome back to audio number seven, establishing routines. The foundation of the mental game and the foundation of consistency come from your ability to be routine. Routine sets the stage for consistency.

A WISE MAN SPEAKS – GOOD TO GREAT

A wise man once said, "The secrets of success are hidden in the routines of our daily lives." The secrets of success are hidden in the routines of our daily lives. And Jim Collins, the author of the one of the greatest-selling business books of all time called *Good To Great*, says, "To be consistent, over time you must be able to describe what you do as a process." Or, to be consistent, over time you must be able to describe what you do as a routine.

WHY ARE ROUTINES IMPORTANT?

Why are routines so important? Routines are important to your softball success because routines allow you to be more comfortable with what you're doing. And when you're more comfortable with what you're doing, you have more confidence. When you have more confidence, you have more consistency. And when you have more consistency, you give yourself the best chance for success.

The best softball players I've ever been around have pre-game and pre-practice routines that are very similar so that they can approach both practice and games the same way. Remember, your opponent is yourself in softball, not the other team. So every day that you put that glove on, every day you lace up those spikes and are going out there to compete, you're competing to be your absolute best. Practice game, national championship game, first game of the year – it doesn't matter. This is about you leaving your legacy in the game of softball one pitch, one day at a time.

WHAT DOES A ROUTINE LOOK LIKE?

What does a pre-game or a pre-practice routine look like? Well, remember the image for our routine is that of an hourglass. An hourglass has a definite start and a definite end to it. So what's an example of a pre-practice routine? Well, in our routine we want to have two or three things that we do to transition ourselves from student into athlete. Just like Superman goes into the phone booth as Clark Kent, Super Nerd, and comes out as Superman, you want to do the same thing. You want to go into your phone booth, aka your locker room, as the super student. And you want to come out the super softball player. And how you do that is to have a specific routine that you follow.

EXAMPLES OF ROUTINES

For example, a lot of players I work with will use their cell phones as a critical part of their routine. When they walk in the locker room, the first thing they do is turn off their cell phones because when you turn off that cell phone, it is life-changing. You're saying: "Goodbye, Mom and Dad. Goodbye, significant others. Goodbye, school. Hello, softball – the game I love to play."

And you see softball and use softball as an escape from the pressures of being a young woman. And you just get to go play. So when the cell phone is off, on is the softball player.

CHANGE YOUR CLOTHES & MENTALITY

The next thing you do is you change your clothes. And as you change out of your street clothes and change into your softball uniform, you're changing into being the ultimate softball player. Very much like a UFC fighter that I work with will change out of a suit into his fight gear to go get in the cage and go to battle, your battle happens on the field.

When you change from street clothes, off come the jeans and there goes the test you've got to take later. Off comes the sweatshirt, and there goes the challenge you're having at home or in your relationships. As you leave that stuff in the locker or in your bag or in your car, you're letting go of what we call your "real self" – your "student self." And you become the ultimate softball player, where you allow yourself to act differently than how you feel.

So if you've had a bad day that day, leave it in the locker and use softball as an escape from reality. Don't let softball bring pressure. Softball should bring pleasure. There's enough pressure in life to perform. Let softball be pleasure, in that it's a game that you go out and love to play, and you have a specific routine you use to get you in the right mindset to have a peak performance.

USE THE SHOES

Cell phone off, change the clothes. The third thing you do is what we call "use the shoes." And this may be the only thing that you do. But you use the shoes, in that when you lace up your spikes, you lock in your focus. And as you lace up those spikes, the last thing you're saying to yourself is what your mission that day is.

Then you get big, you go on that field with great energy, and you compete as hard as you can for the two, three, four, five, eight hours that you're out there. And then, at the end of practice, when the spikes come off and the uniform comes off, you let go of your softball self. Then you change out of your uniform and let go of the softball player who showed up that day, and when you turn the cell phone back on, you become your real self. And you go back to having your student life.

SHOWER IT OFF

Now, if you take a shower after practice or after games, that's also a great way to help yourself come out of that day's softball performance. And if you're a travel player who's playing four, five, six games in a day, I suggest using your shoes to separate yourself from the warrior who's playing and competing. Kick back, put the sandals and the sunglasses on, and start the recovery process person who is going to get some hydration going, get some food in the system - just kick it back and hang with the girls.

Then when it's time to put the spikes back on, you lace them up, you lock it in, you shift your focus and it's go time. So you have routines that you use to create the state and mindset you need be in for performance and to let go of performance after the game. Equally important to have both of those routines.

IMPORTANT TO HAVE POST-GAME ROUTINE

You also have post-practice and post-game routines that allow you to let go of the failure and frustration that come that day in softball and allow you to go back to being who you need to be. We also have pre-pitch routines that we use to help us play pitch to pitch.

VIDEO RESOURCES FOR YOU

Now if you go to briancain.com/softball you're going to see some videos of top college softball players working pre-pitch routines. You'll see when an at-bat starts. We'll use the hourglass image again.

WHEN THE AT-BAT STARTS

The at-bat starts when you have something physical that you do, like put your batting gloves on. If you don't wear batting gloves, use your helmet. You sit down on the bench four people away. You're watching the pitcher. You're going pitch for pitch with that pitcher, using mental imagery and visualizing yourself. Every pitch she throws, she throwing to you. And you make quality contact and hit the ball all over the yard.

Then you go in the hole and get physically loose - on deck, where you're getting your foot down, working your pre-pitch routine. And then you walk big like you're ten feet tall and bulletproof to home plate. When you get to home plate and you're grabbing that bat on the barrel with your dominant hand in a position of power, you clean out the batter's box.

Why do we clean out the batter's box? Because *you* own that batter's box; no one else does. It doesn't matter if you're 10-10 or 0-10 because it's about this pitch. So you clean out that box to take possession. You step out and get your sign from third base. You look at a focal point on your bat or on the home plate. You take a breath. And then you get in the box. As your hands come set by your head or in their set position, you have a final thought, which might be "see it." And then here comes the pitch. You see it. Ball one. And that process and routine repeats itself.

Step out, get the sign from third base, breathe on my focal point, step in the box, hands come set. And I'm saying my final thought, which is "see it."

USE A RELEASE

And let's say you miss your pitch and you're frustrated. Then you've got to go to what we call a release. And a release is something physical that you do to help you clear the past and get back to the present. And a release might be just to wipe the ground with your feet, clean the box again, start that at-bat over. A release might be to undo your batting gloves, let go of that last pitch. It might be to step out and take a practice swing.

Remember our roshambo, rock-paper-scissors analogy. You probably have a release you do already. You just don't consider it a release. So when you do it, it doesn't always have the effect of a release because you don't consider it your release. You do it. You just don't know you're doing it, so you can't do it consistently.

So you work that release, pitch to pitch. Let's say you strike out, because it will happen. You walk back to the dugout. How do you walk back? You walk back big. One of the most frustrating things I see in college and high school softball is women who run back to the dugout, athletes that run back to the dugout.

Now, I understand you've been taught, probably through youth softball, to run back to the dugout because of pace and tempo and to keep the game moving. But do you know what that does to the pitcher when you strike out and sprint back to the dugout? That says, "I don't want any more of you. Let me get back to the dugout." And that gives the pitcher confidence.

So what we practice in the elite programs I work with is that when you strike out, you walk back to the dugout big, you look out to the pitcher's mound, you give her a look, and you let her know that you're coming back up there. And you'll be back up there eight, nine hitters from now, ready to go.

The release then continues when you put your bat away, you put your helmet away, and you sit down on the bench with your batting gloves on and you process the at-bat. What happened? Why did I not have the success that I wanted to have? It's like when an airplane crashes. When an airplane goes down, what do the scientists and researchers go looking for? They go looking for the black box. What's the black box? The black box is the recording of information from the cockpit that lets you and the scientists and researchers know why that plane crashed so we can prevent it from happening again.

And that's exactly what you must do when an at-bat doesn't go your way. Go back to the bench, batting gloves on, process the at-bat, locate the black box, find out why it didn't go the way you wanted it to go. And then when the gloves come off and they go back in your helmet in the helmet rack or they go back in your pocket or back in your bag, then the at-bat is done.

VISUALIZE THE HOURGLASS ROUTINE

Notice the hourglass. At-bat starts, and the gloves go on. At-bat is over when the gloves come off. There is a definite start and end point to it.

Pitchers, you create the same exact process for yourself. Defensively, we have the same process. I step into my circle of focus.

CIRCLE OF FOCUS

As hitters, we have a batter's box that we get in when we're ready. As pitchers, we have a rubber we step on when we're ready. Defensively, we have a circle we draw on the ground, and when we step into that circle, we are ready. Base runners, you know you're ready when you are on the base and you get into your ready position. So you have to have those routines to help you separate from pitch to pitch.

THREE COMPONENTS OF A ROUTINE

And every routine has to have three things that you use.

DEEP BREATH

Number one, most important to get in the present is what?

Take a deep breath.

FINAL THOUGHT

The second thing you have to have: A final thought.

So if I'm a pitcher and I'm throwing screw, maybe I'm going to say "arm-long." If I'm throwing a drop, I might say "turn over," or I say some kind of mental trigger or cue to myself after my breath to keep me consistent as I start my motion to throw that pitch.

Base runners, your final thought might be "see it down." Defensive, your final thought is probably going to be "hit it to me." So it's a deep breath and then the final thought.

A deep breath for the hitter happens before you get in the box. A deep breath for the pitcher happens either before I step on the rubber, as I'm on the rubber before the sign, or as I'm on the rubber after the sign. The deep breath for the base runner happens as I'm on the bag so I don't get tagged out before I get down into my lead. Defensively, the breath happens before you step into your circle.

RELEASE

Now when we talk about releases, you're going to have a physical release that you go to when you recognize that you're not where you need to be. We'll cover that in the next audio. Just know that when you have some negative energy, you're going to need to do something physical to help release the mental. And that's called your release.

So we start to work the hourglass and have specific routines. An hourglass for pre-pitch, for pre-game, for how you wake up in the morning, for how you go to bed at night. And the more consistent you are with those routines, the more consistent you'll be in your performance.

Now, if you're not in the line-up, here's what you want to do. You want to take mental reps. This is critical because in the elite levels of softball – the SEC, the ACC, the Big 12, the Big 10, the Pac 12 - all those players never have sat on the bench. They've always played.

WHAT DO YOU DO WHEN NOT PLAYING?

So when you've always played and now you go to sitting on the bench, being a bench player, or if you're at youth travel ball and move up to the next level or division, it can be the same process. Every level you go, the better and better the players are, the less likely your opportunity is to play every single pitch.

So when you're on the bench, what do you do? You can get bitter, you can feel sorry for yourself, you can complain, and you can switch travel ball programs until you find the one that's so bad that you get play every pitch. Or, you can get better.

Remember, this is about challenging yourself to get to the highest level you can. And if you want more, you must become more. Don't get bitter. Get better. Don't get frustrated. Get fascinated. Don't get turned off. Get turned on by the challenge and become more.

TAKING MENTAL REPS

And here's how you do it when you're on the bench: You pick a player in the game. And every time her position comes up in the line-up, you grab your bat and your batting gloves, and you go down to the other end of the dugout, and you take a mental at-bat.

You stand up in the dugout, you watch the pitcher throw, and then you get your foot down and work the routine. So you're practicing your routine and you're visualizing yourself hitting while you're in the dugout.

Now, you're not taking a live swing because you don't want to kill somebody. But I have worked with teams that have dugouts big enough where they do get a live swing in there in the mental at-bat station.

Let's say your player is a shortstop. There's a ground ball hit to the shortstop up the middle, and she moves to her left and makes the play. You're then going to close your eyes and visualize yourself in the dugout making that same play.

Well, let's say she's on first base and there's a ball thrown in the dirt, drop ball. She takes off, beats the throw to second base, gets the free base on a ball in the dirt. HUGE PLAY! You then close your eyes in the dugout and visualize yourself coming off the base, seeing that ball in the dirt, and going ahead and then diving headfirst in second base, beating the throw and getting that stolen base.

You see, taking mental reps with a player at the plate, in the circle, defensively and on the bases is essential to you staying in the game. You work your deep breath, you work your routine so that when you get the chance to go in and play, you're that much closer to being game-ready.

So the routine is going to give you that layer of consistency while you're playing. The routine is going to give you that something to do to stay sharp when you're not in the line-up. The routine is going to give you the best chance for success because it's going to give you the best chance to be consistent. And the more precise and detailed you are in your routines, the better your chance for success.

SUPERSTITION vs. ROUTINE

Here's a caution statement: Remember that it's about execution, competition and winning. But winning is a by-product of working the process. And your process is your routine. I have a lot of players who get very, very stuck in routines. They become superstitious. Superstition is: If I don't do "this," I can't win. Routine is: I'm going to find a way to win, but by doing this I give myself the best chance to win. If I can't work my routine because I get to a game late or I can't work my routine because of some outside circumstance, I'm able to say "so what, next pitch," trust my training, go out there and go to battle.

When you can, you work the routine. When you can't, you trust your training and you pick up the routine where you can, which is usually at the plate, and you go to battle. You go to battle. You win pitches - and winning championships will take care of itself.

TRUST YOUR ROUTINES

Trust your routines. And trust your routines by working on them every day in practice. What you practice, what you train will show up in competition. Make sure you practice your routines just like you practice the game. This is Brian Cain, your Peak Performance and Mental Conditioning Coach, helping you to become a machine of consistency through a routine, which will allow you to become a machine of championship rings.... BOOM!

Establishing Routines for Consistent Softball Performance

REVIEW SHEET

1. The secrets of success are hidden in the _____ _____.

2. Routines allow you to become more comfortable with what you are doing which leads to confidence which leads to consistency which leads to giving yourself the best chance for _____.

3. The best players have pre-_____ and pre-practice routines that are similar so that you can approach each the same way, because your opponents are _____ and _____.

4. They also have _____ routines that let us play pitch to pitch.

5. When we talk about routines, we want to use the image of an _____ so that we have a definite _____ and _____ for each pitch, inning, at-bat, practice and game.

6. When does an at-bat start? When you put your _____. When is an at-bat over? When you take the _____ or helmet off.

7. Inside of your routine you want to have a place where you take a (1) _____ on a focal point, have a (2) final _____ and a (3) _____ so that you can stay consistent in your approach.

www.briancain.com

8. If you are not in the line-up, you want to take _____ with the person who is playing your position.

9. Be sure that you visit www.briancain.com/softball to watch the routine videos that are available so you can see top college softball players and ESPN announcers talking about the at-bat and pitching routines.

RECOGNIZING YOUR SIGNAL LIGHTS
GO GREEN

Well, we're now going into extra innings. This is audio number eight, "Recognizing Your Signal Lights – Let's Go Green."

RECOGNITION IS ESSENTIAL FOR SUCCESS

You see, when you go through the mental game, it comes down to your ability to recognize where you're at and go green. What does that mean? Well, put your hands out in front of you right now. No, come on – really. Put your hands in front of you like you're grabbing a steering wheel and you're driving that car of your dreams.

GRAB THE WHEEL AND HOLD ON

And as you're driving that car of your dreams down the highway to excellence, you come to a signal light. And if the signal light is green, what you do? You go. If the signal is red, what do you do? You stop. Well, what if that signal light's yellow? What do you do? What do you do? I bet half the room said, "Speed up." Half the room said, "Slow down." You're both right.

That's what happens in softball. When you're going really, really good, you don't need the mental game. You're in green lights - just play, baby.

WE LIVE IN YELLOW LIGHTS

When you play softball, probably 10% of the time you're in green, 10% of the time you're in red, 80% of the time you're going to battle with your mental skills because you are in yellow lights. You see, in yellow lights it's not going really good and it's not going really bad. You're battling to go pitch by pitch and play to the best of your ability. And the greater the stakes, the higher the competition, the closer that yellow light gets to a red.

If we go back through your skeleton files, we know number six is your ability to have routines.

Number seven is your ability to recognize your signal lights. And if you recognize your signal lights, you can then manage yourself through emotional, mental, physical management skills to get you into a peak state where you'll play your best.

AWARENESS AND CONTROL

You see, the ability to recognize where you're at mentally and emotionally and physically when competing is known as having awareness of your signal lights. And when you can recognize your signal lights, what you're aware of, you can control. What you're unaware of will control you.

MASTERS OF THE MENTAL GAME

Now, remember in our first track I talked about a gentleman that has been a mentor to me, a guy named Harvey Dorfman? I had the amazing opportunity to be brought up under the tutelage of the greatest sports psychologist on the planet, Dr. Ken Ravizza. He was my mentor for two years at Cal State Fullerton and remains so to this day.

Ken wrote the greatest book ever written, *Heads-Up Baseball*. I also got to know Harvey Dorfman. Harvey wrote the book *The Mental Game of Baseball*. And Harvey taught me something about awareness that I wanted to share with you.

He said, "It only takes three things for you, as a softball player, to change your performance and make performance improvements."

Number one is: You have awareness.

Number two is: You have a strategy.

Number three is: You put the strategy into action.

What Ken talked about with awareness was: How do you recognize your signal lights? How do you communicate about knowing where you're at? And he said: "How you recognize where you're at is through the analogy of having signal lights. When you're good and you're green, you're confident. Where you're yellow, you're just starting to lose it. And when you're in red, you're totally gone. Stick a fork in you, you're done."

Ken talked about how there are three ways to recognize your signal lights:

1. Through your self-talk, how you communicate to yourself.

2. Through your physical feelings, how you feel physically.

3. What situations in softball would trigger your green, yellow or red lights?

So to help build awareness about yourself as a softball player, go ahead and write down what you say to yourself, how you feel and what situations in the game trigger your green, yellow and red lights.

EXAMPLES OF SIGNAL LIGHTS

Now let me give you some examples. When you're in green lights, you might say to yourself, "I got this, I love this, bring it on" – while you might feel physically loose, big, confident, energized. What situations might give you green lights? Making quality contact, a good round of batting practice, following my routine. How I feel physically might be a situation that gives me a green light.

What about yellow lights? My self-talk might be, "I don't know if I can do this, I can't believe I missed that pitch." Physical feelings might be: I start to get a little tight, I start to get a little bit of dry mouth. Situations might be: An umpire makes a bad call, I throw a pitch not nearly where I want to throw it, I lose a fly ball in the sun.

What might be a red light? Red light self-talk: "I suck, I can't do this, why do I even play?" Red light physical feelings: Tired, slow like the game is moving so fast that you're inadequate. Situations: I strike out three times in a game, I make an error, I throw three bad pitches in a row. A red light is a magnified yellow. A yellow is it's just starting, it's like spiraling out of control. A red is that it's completely gone, and you're done.

So what you want to do is develop an awareness so that you can recognize your signal lights by writing down how you talk to yourself, how you feel and what situations trigger your green, yellow and red lights.

Now that you have a better understanding of your signal lights, let me give you three tips about how you might be able to better recognize what player you become when you struggle. Well, just like we did when you were going really good with the confidence resume, when you were playing your best, what were you doing – reliving those best performances. We want to do the same with the negative performances, right? We want to learn from the good and the bad.

GOOD & BAD, NEVER GOOD OR BAD

As an elite-level softball player and a coach, do not evaluate your performance as good or bad. Evaluate your performance as good AND bad. Your performance is not good or bad. It's good AND bad. Every day you play, there's going to be some good. Every day you play, there's going to be some bad. So we evaluate as good AND bad.

PRAYER, PRIMAL, PERFECT

When you struggle in softball, you're going to become one of three players: primal, prayer or perfect. And this comes right out of *Heads-Up Baseball* with Dr. Ken Ravizza, my mentor.

If you're the primal player, you become the cavewoman. You become the player that tries to swing harder, throw faster, do more – cavewoman. Softball doesn't work that way. You can't get pissed and try to do more. When you do that, it's like getting in quicksand. What happens when you're in quicksand? You fight harder and you sink faster. And that's what happens to the primal pitcher or the primal player when she gets in red lights.

What about prayer? I hope that they give me a pitch that I can hit. Please, somebody guide this ball over home plate and let it be a strike. You start praying that there's an outside factor that's going to come in to help you hit the ball hard or to help you execute a pitch. When you start praying and hoping – really, this is not a religious connotation here. This is a hoping. I'm the hoping player. I hope that it works for me. Well, you're praying and you're hoping, and you're not going out there to impose your will and play your game.

Don't a prayer player. Be a premier player, a peak performing player.

Do not be a perfect player. You see, perfect is the third "P" of the three players you can become when you get into yellow or red lights. I've got to make the perfect pitch. Got to make the perfect pitch here. Ball one. Oh, but I just missed on the corner. It was perfect.

Or, I've got to get the perfect pitch for a hit. And I took that one - it was close but it wasn't perfect. Strike one. And if you're trying to be perfect, you can't win. Perfection doesn't exist.

CAN'T WALK ON WATER

I was with the University of Houston softball team. We were playing Oklahoma State in NCAA Super Regional before the 2011 NCAA College World Series. And our players were trying to be a little bit too perfect. So master of the mental game, head coach Kyla Holas, what does she do? She brings out a cooler, fills it with water, has all of her players take their shoes and socks off and says, "Step inside of this cooler and let's see if you can walk on water." Not one player could walk on water. And neither can you. And what does that mean? That means you cannot be perfect and play championship softball. Focus on being excellent, not perfect. Perfection kills, excellence wins.

Don't be primal. Don't be prayer. Don't be perfect. Be a premier, prime-time, peak performer - trusting your routines, playing one pitch at a time, living in the present, focusing on the process, staying positive.

CHECK IN

Now if you see a teammate or somebody who you think is getting taken over by yellow and then maybe red lights, there is a term that we use: Check in. If you as a player hear a coach or someone saying, "Hey, check in - check in, Brian - check in," that refers to checking in on your signal lights. Get a good breath; use your release because I think you're getting away from what we want, which is process and getting into results.

So the buzzword we use for you to recognize your signal lights is "check in." Anytime someone says "check in," you might be focused on things outside of your control. You need to lock back in on what you can control because that's where champions live.

ATW – AWARENESS TO WIN

Today, your mission is to become more aware and develop that ATW, Awareness To Win, that's needed in softball about the game. Most importantly, be aware of yourself in performance because if you want more from softball and if you want to perform better, you must become more and you must become better. And that happens through being able to recognize your signal lights in performance and go green.

Recognizing Your Signal Lights Go Green

REVIEW SHEET

1. The ability to recognize where you are mentally, physically and emotionally when competing is also known as having awareness and being able to recognize your _____.

2. What you are _____ of you can control; what you are _____ of will control you.

3. Harvey Dorfman, who wrote *The Mental Game of Baseball,* taught me that anytime an athlete wants to make a performance change she has to have three things:

    (1) A_____ of what needs to change (2) S_____ to change (3) Put the s_____ into _____.

4. What are some ways that you recognize when you are confident and in green lights? How do you recognize when you start to lose it and get into yellow and then beat yourself by playing in red lights?

    Green Yellow Red

    A = Self-talk

    B = Physical Feelings

    C = Situations

5. When you struggle in softball, you will often become one of three players:

(1) P_____

(2) P_____

(3) P_____

6. The term "_____ in" refers to your checking in on your signal lights and getting a good breath, but also on shifting your attention from what if (results) to what is (process) and onto what is important now. A good time for a coach or teammate to say "check in" would be when he or she sees something happen that could trigger yellow or red lights or cause you to focus on the wrong thing. Use the term "check in" to remind a teammate to get back to green after something outside of your _____ happens.

RELEASE YOUR MENTAL BRICKS & REFOCUS ON WIN
SO WHAT, NEXT PITCH!

Thanks for staying with me to day nine. I'm really proud of the fact that you have committed to being your absolute best and going to work on yourself first and going to work on your mental game, because when you work on your mental game, you become more. And when you become more, you will get more. Absolutely, positively guaranteed.

4RIP3 REVIEW

Let's review with your right-hand skeleton files. You know you've got to live and compete in the present and you get there by taking a deep breath.

Focus on the process, not the outcome. And the process is going through school and life one step at a time, playing softball one pitch at a time.

We always work to control what we can control. The acronym that we have to remind us of what we can control is our APE.

We talk about location number four, being positive. Being positive means turning have to into want to, haven't done it yet, compared to what, attitude of gratitude – being positive.

Number five is your mental imagery.

Number six is making sure that you have routines. Inside your routine you recognize where you're at, then you release and refocus. And that's how you dominate the day.

RELEASE AND REFOCUS

Well, right now, in audio number nine, we're going to talk about your ability to release and refocus. But in order for you to release, you first have to recognize that you are in a yellow or red light. You see, if you're in green, there's nothing to release. You simply refocus on the next pitch.

If you recognize that you've got yellow lights or you recognize that you've got red lights, you must have a physical release that you go to in order to help you get to the next pitch.

EXAMPLES OF RELEASES

As a hitter, if you need to have a release, you might as well use cleaning out the batter's box because that's what you do to start your at-bat. So in an at-bat, you might need to release an umpire's call, something that's said from the stands or the last pitch that you missed – just go ahead and clean out the batter's box and reset your mentality back to being in the present moment.

And if you're a pitcher, you probably do this already. You get the ball back from the catcher and you clean up the landing area where your foot lands when you're pitching or right in front of the pitching rubber. And as you clean up that area, you release the last pitch and refocus on the next one. When you walk to the back of the circle, you may also go back and pick up some chalk or wipe the back of the circle or look at second base. As you're looking at second base, you take a deep breath. And that helps you to release that last pitch.

Now if you go to www.briancain.com/softball I'll show you a video of a pitcher from Coastal Carolina University. You're going to see her walk to the back of the circle, draw a circle and press a button, which is essentially her reset button. And you see an example of a pitcher using a release.

I'll also show you a video of Melissa Gregson, the 2011 Conference USA Player of the Year from the University of Houston in a super regional against Oklahoma State, where she swings through a pitch. She'll step out of the box, get her sign from third base, reach down and wipe the dirt as her release. So you'll see those two examples.

But what you first have to do before you can release is recognize. So you learn to recognize. And then, inside your routine, you use that release when you are in a yellow or red light.

PRE-DETERMINED RELEASE

You must have a pre-determined, pre-practiced physical release that you go to that helps you to mentally release the last pitch and refocus back to what's important now. And what's important now is always the next pitch. So in practice, have a station, a tee station, where you hit, you get a swing, you step out, you practice your release, you refocus and you take another swing. And just the part of that station in practice is for you to take out the component of your routine where you're working on your release and working on your ability to refocus.

SO WHAT

We talked about using the verbal cue, "check in," to help you recognize if someone saw that you were in yellow or red lights. Now the term we use for release is "so what." And the term we use for refocus is "next pitch." So the term, "so what, next pitch" - which happens to be the title of my second book following the number one best seller, *Toilets, Bricks, Fish Hooks and Pride: The Peak Performance Toolbox Exposed* – the term, "so what, next pitch" really means release, refocus.

Let me ask you this. As an elite-level softball player, do you have to have every single call go your way to win? Well, the obvious answer is "no." So when a call doesn't go your way, just say, "so what, next pitch" and play the next pitch.

There's no need to gripe, no need to complain. You can get pissed and release, but you only have about ten seconds to release before you've got to play the next pitch. But you better get over it, and you better move on because the next pitch is coming.

EXAMPLES OF RELEASES

So what are some good, physical ways that you can have a release in a yellow or red light to get back to green?

Well, one is finding a focal point and taking a good, deep breath – just like you do to refocus. Your focal point's probably on your bat, or on the rubber if you are a pitcher; and when you look at your focal point, that's where you take that deep breath.

RELEASE FOCAL POINTS

You want to have a focal point and a deep breath as a part of your release. Now as a hitter, I often talk about going to the left field or right field foul pole. As a pitcher, always turn your back to home plate and look at second base because when you release, you want to have your energy away from where you need to compete. So hitters look away from the pitcher and at a foul pole and pitchers look at second base.

RELEASES FOR HITTERS

Another way to use a physical release to help release the mental is to use your batting gloves. Unstrap your batting gloves, put the bat down between your legs, re-strap your batting gloves back on and re-strap yourself to the next pitch.

RELEASES FOR PITCHERS

As a pitcher, get the ball back and just wipe the dirt off the rubber. As you wipe the dirt off the rubber, you're wiping away that last pitch.

RELEASES FOR DEFENSE

As a defensive player, just clean the dirt or the grass of the area in front you. As you clean that and wipe that away, you're wiping yourself back to the next pitch. Another one you can do is take off your glove, defensively. And as you smooth out the dirt or the grass in front of you, you take that deep breath, looking down at the ground, and then put your glove back on, pull up your sternum, get big and lock in for the next pitch.

So we talked a lot about those releases and refocus in-game. And you're always refocusing back to what's your plan for that next pitch. Well, post-practice routines are a great way to release at the end of practice.

POST-PRACTICE RELEASE

We talked about coming out of your hourglass and taking off your spikes and your uniform, leaving the stress in the locker and using the shower or your cell phone as a way to turn yourself back into the student, because you have to be able to walk away and separate softball from life.

Remember, softball is what you do - it is not who you are. Don't beat the ever-living, ever-loving hell out of yourself if you are not playing well. Doing that only makes the problem bigger.

MENTAL BRICKS

If you don't release after practice, what happens is you start carrying mental bricks. And those mental bricks are just like physical bricks. Now a physical brick - you could carry that for five seconds. It's no big deal. But carry that physical brick with your arm out straight in front of you for 10, 20 or 30 seconds, a minute, two minutes, five minutes, ten minutes, a half-hour. The next thing you know your arm's going to fall off.

You do the same thing in softball. You carry mental bricks when you make a mistake, and you don't learn from it and let it go. Make a mistake, learn from it, let it go, move onto the next pitch. Don't carry mental bricks, because when you do, they will hold you down just like physical bricks do. Being able to separate the last pitch to the next pitch is critical to your success in softball.

BE COACHABLE

What does it mean to be coachable? It is being able to see coaching, constructive criticism and failure as a compliment and not an attack. Failure and coaching are compliments that say, "You're in the right place, and we believe you can be better." It's not an attack that you're not good enough. You've got to understand those two differences.

PERSONAL ATTACK vs. PROFESSIONAL COACH

And I see a lot of young softball players get caught up in the personal attack versus the lesson that can be learned. You have to separate softball from who you are and what you do. Softball is not who you are. Softball is what you do. Be very clear in those two things. Your self-worth as a young woman is not tied to your batting average, not tied to your ERA and not tied to wins and losses. It's tied to your commitment to excellence, who you are in the path of who you're going to become, and how you live your values.

Separating professional feedback and coaching and not taking them as a personal attack is critical to your growth.

Champions thirst for professional feedback about their performance. Coaching is not personal criticism. Understanding the difference between the professional and the personal is going to help you a lot when you get out of softball and get into life. This is what we're trying to create - that success mentality - so when you get out there in the real world you can take that constructive criticism as a compliment and keep climbing that ladder.

RECOGNIZING GREEN vs. RED

So when you recognize you're in green lights, there's nothing to release. Refocus on the next pitch. Refocusing means you come up with a plan for that next pitch. If you recognize you have yellow lights or red lights, you go to your physical release that's been pre-determined, pre-practiced. And before the next pitch, you know what your release is going to be. You let it go, take a deep breath and then you get back into your routine, your pre-pitch routine of a breath on a focal point, your final thought. And you win that next pitch.

THE 4RIP3 SYSTEM

So here you have it. The 4RIP3 System. You just learned the last of the four "R's." Inside your routine, you recognize where you're at. If you're in red or yellow, you release. If you're in green, you refocus. You use mental imagery as a part of your daily preparation and also preparation at night before you go to sleep. And you live in that present moment, focus on the process and stay positive. And if you work the 4RIP3 System, you will absolutely, positively guaranteed, give yourself the best chance for success in this great game of softball.

Release Your Mental Bricks & Refocus on WIN - So What, Next Pitch!

REVIEW SHEET

1. Inside of your routine, when you recognize that you are in a yellow or red light, you must have a pre-determined physical _____ that you go to that helps you to mentally release the last pitch and _____ back to what's important now. What's important now is always the next _____.

2. We used the verbal "C_____ I_____" for recognize; you must now think "S__ W_____" as your release and "N_____ P_____" as your refocus cue. The term "S__ W_____, N_____ P_____" really means r_____ and r_____.

3. What are some physical ways that you can release a yellow or red light and get back to a green?

    (1) Finding a focal point and taking a _____.

    (2) Undoing your b_____ and restrapping them to refocus you to the next pitch and get a deep breath.

    (3) Wiping the pitcher's _____ as a way to wipe away the last pitch.

    (4) Taking off your _____ and smoothing out the dirt in the infield or the grass, and then taking a deep breath and putting your glove back on to get to the next pitch.

4. Using your post-practice routine is a great way to release at the end of practice. It will help you leave softball at softball, to be able to walk away and leave the good and _____ from the day behind you and to focus on what you need to do as a student.

5. Being able to see coaching and constructive criticism as a c_____ vs. an attack is an example of being able to separate softball from who you are to _____.

6. Being able to separate from professional vs. _____ will help you a LOT when you get into a professional career. It will enable you to grow and take constructive criticism to get better vs. take it as an attack and get bitter.

7. When you recognize that you are in green lights, you should go right to _____ on the next pitch. Refocusing means that you come up with a plan for the next pitch.

8. When you recognize that you are in red or yellow lights and are carrying the metaphorical mental _____ that will weigh you down if you carry it for more than a few seconds, you must be able to release that _____ and get to the next pitch.

9. If you recognize that you have yellow or red lights, you have to r_____ before you play the next pitch. There are many things you can do as a release; the biggest one for softball is taking a releasing deep breath before you take your refocusing deep breath on your focal point to lock into the next pitch.

THE COMPOUND EFFECT, TYING IT ALL TOGETHER AND GETTING TO WORK

Well, congratulations on making it all the way to the finish line, which is actually the starting line as you're going to see. This is day ten. It's not the end; it's just the beginning of the new you and the beginning of you going out and playing your best when it means the most, which is every single day, every single pitch.

THIS IS THE START, NOT THE END

You see, if you're going to grow, you must grow by doing a little a lot – not a lot a little. Mental toughness is like a muscle. And it must be worked if it's going to grow.

THE COMPOUND EFFECT

If I offer an audience of 1000 people a check for $3 million or a penny that doubled every day for only one month, over 90% of the people are going to grab the $3 million. They want the short-term fix. You see, most people make the mistake of putting off what they want most for what they want in the moment. BUT NOT YOU! You have stayed committed to the process of putting off what you want in the moment for what you want most, which is to become the most mentally tough softball player you can be.

And if you took that penny, one cent, on day one and it doubled every day, at 29 days you've got $2.5 million, at 30 days you finally pass the other people in the room, and you've got $5 million. But that 31-day month gives you over $10 million by taking a penny and doubling it every day. That's called "the compound effect."

The compound effect says that what you do every day compounds and makes you the person that you are going to become. Your mental game is going to compound. Your performance is going to grow with the daily investment of that penny, reviewing this book, reading *The Daily Dominator* and the daily investment of watering the bamboo. You must understand the compound effect, and you must understand watering the bamboo.

WATER THE BAMBOO

There are over 1,500 species of bamboo. But the great timber bamboo is the most fascinating of all. If you plant great timber bamboo and water it every day for one year, you get no growth. The second year, water it every day, and you get no growth. The third year, water it every single day, and you get no growth.

In the fourth year, if you keep watering that bamboo every day, you're going to get 90 feet of growth in just 60 days – the strongest, most durable bamboo on the planet. Ninety feet in 60 days, but no growth for three years. The magic of the great timber bamboo is in sticking to the process of watering it every day. In year four it grows 90 feet in 60 days. But does it really?

YOU JUST NEVER KNOW

I think it grows 90 feet in three years and 60 days. You see, you never know when you're going to catch that growth spurt. You never know when you're going to explode and become the softball player and the athlete that you want to be.

You've got to stick to the process, keep putting the compound effect to work for you by doing a little a lot every single day by having simple yet powerful daily routines and processes, and keep watering that bamboo.

The challenge here is for you to listen to the 4RIP3 audio on a consistent basis. Every time you listen to these audios, you're going to be in a different place personally, you're going to be a different woman, you're going to grow and mature and get more out of listening to these. We learn best through repetition. That's why this is not the finish line of your mental conditioning program - this is the starting line. This is the start of you becoming the best "you" that you can be.

AVOID CAM'S MISTAKE

Don't the make the mistake that my friend Cam made. Remember Roger Bannister? Cam got the same, exact training program that Roger Bannister had. And on day one of the 100 days before Bannister ran the sub-four-minute mile, he ran a test race and ran a 4:12.

My friend Cam ran the same test 100 days before the big race that he wanted to go under 4:00, the same as Bannister, and he blew Bannister away by running a 4:06. He thought he was in better shape than Bannister, so he took some days off, didn't do what Bannister did, showed everyone Bannister's program - and then went out on race day and ran a 4:06. He didn't get any better. Why?

CAM'S MISTAKE

He had the program. He didn't use the program. He knew what to do but he did not do what he knew. Don't make that same mistake. And know that the times here are not 100% accurate. I made this story up to teach you a very important point about DOING WHAT YOU KNOW and PUTTING THIS PROGRAM IN YOUR HANDS INTO ACTION... YES, I AM SHOUTING!!!

I get fired up when it comes to your performance!

THE START STOPS MOST PEOPLE

It's the start that stops most people. And you've made it this far, so you have started. Now, you must continue to grow and water that bamboo.

4RIP3 REVIEW

Know that mental toughness is a skill and it helps you to be at your best when it means the most, that this game of softball knows who deserves to win and will reward those who do what they're supposed to do, and that this game is bigger than us all.

The goal of this program, the goal of the game of softball, is to train you how to be a successful woman in life. When you find your big reason "why," you will find a way how. And know that those three steps to performance – awareness, strategy and action – are as easily implemented as if you asked yourself, on a scale of one to ten, "Where am I at compared to where I want to be? And what do I have to start, stop and continue to get to where I want to go?"

The goal of the 4RIP3 System is to help you play one pitch at a time. Reinforcing of the process is more important than the end result, and your goal must be in your control because you have control over the process – never the outcome.

Mentally tough athletes focus on what they want to do – not what they're trying to avoid.

The best team never wins. It's always the team who plays the best.

Practice with a purpose and be on a mission because practice makes permanent.

Change softball practice into softball training.

Know that there are four stages of commitment to what you do: Have a job, do work, have a career or be on a mission. And you want to have a mission for every day - a goal and purpose and a plan for each day that you go to train because when you have quality practice and step up every day, there is no step-up in the big game.

The key to learning is to totally immerse yourself and do a little a lot – not a lot a little. That's why it is so critical that you read my book *The Daily Dominator* every morning as part of your start-up routine.

That's why you read the Monday e-mail that you can sign up for at briancain.com/monday. And you listen to these audios on a consistent basis.

Now you've gone through the four stages of acceptance. I'm sure you started off with number one, "Hey, this ain't for me." Number two, "This is OK for others." Number three, "Hmm. I'll try it." And now, hopefully, number four, as you continue to progress, you'll say: "I can't believe I did it any other way. I used to focus so much on the things I couldn't control. And now I just lock in on what I can. And it's changed my life."

Know that there are three steps to memorizing anything. And you can memorize anything. You don't have a good or bad memory; you have a trained or untrained memory. You can do anything if you have the right training. And the training to memorize anything is to create three things: Location, picture and meaning.

We talked to you about the right-hand skeleton files for our 4RIP3 System. So stand up, take your right hand. Touch yourself on the top of the head. Live in the present by taking a deep breath. Now touch yourself on the nose, focus on the process. One step, one pitch at a time. Control what you can control is number three, and all you can control is your APE. Number four, your ribs, be positive. That means turn have-to's into want-to's, haven't done it yet, compared to what and have an attitude or gratitude.

Number five, your abs, is the mental imagery visualizing yourself playing at your best. Number six, your hips, is to have routines to be consistent. Number seven is your knees, recognize your signal lights. Number eight is your shins, release and flush it. Number nine is those green feet, refocus on the next pitch, which helps you with number ten, which is to dominate the day.

And you dominate the day every day with that 4RIP3 System. And you know that the most important day of your softball career is today.

Don't count the days. Make the days count and know that today plus today plus today equals your season and your career. And the time is now. The place is here.

You've got that bank account. It's giving you 86,400 seconds a day not to spend. But to do what? To invest into your career, invest into your personal development and invest in this great game of softball.

Know that when I walk up and see you in practice, I'm going to say, "What are you working on today?" And you should have a plan and a mission. Setting pre-practice goals helps you to get in that present moment for the day and improve that training session.

And we know there are three special ways that we train ourselves to stay in the present moment. We use the concentration grids and go one number at a time. We use the 5-4-3-2-1 relaxation and focus exercise and go one breath at a time, and the inhale/exhale exercise to keep our mind in the moment. By using concentration grids, you train yourself to focus for a longer period of time. Recognize when your mind wanders out of the present and pull it back. Keep track of your time on the concentration grids because measurement equals motivation. And when you breathe, you're training that relaxation response and your ability to focus so that if you want to take that deep breath – 3-2, bases loaded – and pull yourself in the present, you must be able to do that off the field.

We talked about the process giving you the best chance for success. The process, controlling what you can control and that your goal must be where? That's right, in your control.

The process is those steps that you take to get to the top of that staircase – remember that picture. And the process is about competing with yourself in the game – never your opponent.

We talked about the law of averages in the process. There are only four things can happen when you play softball. You can play well and win. You can play well and lose. You can play lousy and win. You can play lousy and lose. But we're trying to play well to give ourselves the best chance to win.

Memorize the seven ways that you beat the game. This is with our left hand. Remember those pictures. Zero was make no errors. One was score first. Two was execute two out of three first pitches for a strike. Three was to hold your opponent to three runs or less. Four was to have 54% quality at-bats. Five was score five runs or more. And "W" was win the freebie war because free bases lead to runs, which lead to wins, which lead to championships. Your job as a hitter is to have a quality at-bat. Your job as pitcher is to execute quality pitches.

Winning softball games is a by-product of working the process. The way you stand for the National Anthem is part of the process. How organized your locker is and how you manage your time are parts of the process. Maybe the most important part of the process and the most important part of this entire program are your two critical lists of what you can and what you cannot control. Review those on a daily basis and remind yourself to focus only on what you can control.

Be positive. Again, turn those have-to's into want-to's. Focus on what you want and not what you're trying to avoid. Know that you can do anything. You just haven't done it - what? Yet.

Positive people have that attitude of gratitude, and they write down one thing they're thankful for every day. They know it could get worse – compared to what.

They build that attitude of gratitude and perspective by creating a perspective poster. They train the voice inside of their heads that they listen to by having a confidence resume and writing out confidence conditioning statements.

Remember the Indian chief story? The red wolf or the green wolf. Which one's going to win the battle is the one that you train. It's called the battle of self-talk. Confidence conditioning statements - write them down, review them on a routine basis. Your confidence resume - review it on a routine basis.

Know that "E" plus "R" equals "O," the events plus your response equal the outcome. Positive people know that will beats skill in softball and that the best team's never going to win; it will always be the team that plays the best.

What did Bannister teach us about softball? There are no physical barriers, just mental barriers to overcome. Get that confidence resume down. Start writing down those reasons to believe in yourself, because you're going to the canvas. And when you're on the canvas after getting knocked down, you can pick yourself up quicker and easier by knowing why you're good and why you should succeed both as an individual, as a coach and as a program.

Get big and fake it 'til you make it.

Know the big ABC's: Act big, Breathe big and Commit big.

Use mental imagery and visualization. You know that you do it already without even knowing it. But now use it. Use it and enhance it by watching highlight videos of yourself and other people on TV, on YouTube, and then play those videos of yourself performing that way in your mind.

Do relaxation before you do imagery because when you get into that relaxed state, it sets the stage for clear and vivid imagery that goes to work on the subconscious mind that runs the computer that makes you do what you do. When doing imagery, use as many senses as possible. And know that doing imagery is different than just thinking about softball. Thinking about softball happens all the time. Imagery is a purpose-driven activity like going to the weight room.

Know that mind control leads to body control which leads to skill control. If you're going to be able to execute a pitch, you've got to be able to repeat your mechanics. In order to repeat your mechanics, you've got to repeat your mental mechanics.

Why is imagery effective? Because the brain processes information, whether you vividly imagine it or physically do it, with the same psycho-neuromuscular pathways.

And there are four - that's right, four - steps to effective mental imagery. Relaxation, confidence conditioning, mental recall, mental rehearsal. And you've got those audios in this program to take yourself through them.

Softball hitters should be doing active mental imagery when they're four hitters away. Pitchers should be doing active mental imagery as a part of their routine, where they see themselves executing the pitch they want to throw. See the lane of where you're throwing that softball.

Again, when you do imagery, apply the rule of doing a little a lot – not a lot a little. Better to do five minutes a day than 20 minutes once a week. Do mental imagery as a part of your pre-game and pre-pitch routines, as well as the night before.

Now when we're talking about routines, know that the secrets of success are hidden in the routines of our daily lives. Routines allow you to become more comfortable with what you're doing, which leads to confidence, which leads to consistency, which leads to your best chance for success.

The best players have pre-game and pre-practice routines that are similar so that they can approach each the same way, because your opponent is always yourself and the game. They have pre-pitch routines that let them play pitch to pitch.

When we talk about routines, use the image of an hourglass so that we have a definite start and end time for each pitch, each inning, each at-bat and each game to help us stay consistent.

When does an at-bat start for you? Is it when you put your gloves or helmet on? When is an at-bat over for you? Is it when you take them off? Be able to describe that.

Inside your routine, have a place where you take a deep breath on a focal point, have a final thought and a release so you can stay consistent in your approach.

If you're not in the line-up, you want to take mental reps with the person who's in your position. Mental reps are huge for you to stay positive and consistent when you're not getting the playing time that you want because you're not in the line-up or because you're injured.

Be sure that you visit briancain.com/softball and watch the videos that are on there so you get a visual example of the routines and releases that we've been talking about in this program. You'll also see some video clips that I've taken off of TV from the College World Series and NCAA tournament, where coaches and athletes I work with are talking about aspects of the mental game, like flushing it, mental bricks, controlling what you can control. It's all in there. They may not even know they're saying it because, ultimately, as you condition yourself and train yourself with this program, you'll start to speak and think that way as well.

Know that what you're aware of you can control. What you're unaware of will control you. And your ability to recognize where you're at mentally, physically, emotionally while competing is having awareness and knowing your signal lights. How do you learn your signal lights? You learn your signal lights by knowing that green means go, yellow means, "I better slow down or speed up" and red means stop. And I recognize my signal lights in one of three ways: my self-talk, my physical feelings or the situations that happen.

When you struggle in softball you often become one of three players: primal, prayer or perfect. You've got to recognize which one of those you are and have a release to get you back to green.

The term "check in" refers to you checking in on your signal lights. It means: Hey, I think you're in yellow or red. Get a good, deep breath and shift your attention away from "what if" or results and put it on "what is," which is process, and what's important now.

So when you see one of your teammates who's struggling or it looks like they're focusing on something outside of their control, use the word "check in" to get them to check in on their signal lights. Now if they check in and see that they're in yellow or red lights, they must have a pre-determined, practiced physical release that they go to that helps them to mentally release the last pitch and refocus back to what's important now. We use the verbal, "Check in - hey, check in here" to help recognize.

Then we use the verbal "so what" to release. And then "next pitch" to help you refocus on that next pitch. So the term "so what, next pitch" really means release, refocus.

Now what are some physical ways that you can release a yellow or red light and get back to a green? Find a focal point, take a deep breath, undo your batting gloves, re-strap them on and re-strap your mentality of the next pitch.

As a pitcher, wipe the rubber, wipe away that last pitch, get to the next one. Defensively, take off your glove, kick some dirt, take a deep breath looking at a focal point of a foul pole, lock back into the next pitch.

Using your pre-practice and your post-practice routines are great ways to help you separate school and softball, student and athlete. And know that every day is not going to be good or bad. It's going to be good AND bad. There's always good and bad with every day.

Learn to be coachable. See constructive criticism as a compliment versus an attack on you. Softball's not who you are. Softball is what you do, and those are different. You are not your batting average. Learning to separate professional and personal is going to be huge because when you get into a professional career, it's going to help you grow and take constructive criticism to get better versus taking it and getting bitter. And in my professional career, I see a lot more people who take constructive criticism and get bitter instead of wanting to get better. Don't fall into that negative trap.

Again, you're in green lights. And what do you do? You don't need release when you're in green lights. You just refocus on the next pitch. Recognize you're in green and play the next pitch. When you recognize you're in red or yellow and you're carrying that metaphorical mental brick that's going to hold you down, you've got to let that go within a few seconds. Release that brick by doing your physical release and get to that next pitch. If you recognize you've got a yellow or red, release and refocus.

If you want more, you must become more. How you become more is to set five personal development plan goals. Put them on your right hand and memorize them just like you did the seven ways to beat the game with your left hand. For example, let's say on my pinky, I'm going to be disciplined and make my bed every day. Ring finger, I'm going to send a text message to a teammate and pump her up every day. Maybe my middle finger, I'm going to get an extra conditioning session in after we weight train every day for at least ten minutes. Pointer finger, I'm going make sure that I get to bed at least one hour earlier. Thumb, I'm going to be more accountable, and I'm going to learn to say "no" to things that are taking me away from my mission of being an elite-level softball player because you can't do everything. You probably can only do two things at a level of excellence. And that should be softball and school. Everything else you can take care of when those two things are over.

Write down your five personal development plan goals. Take a dry erase marker and write them on your mirror, write them on an index card. Put them somewhere where you can see them every day. You've got a short window of opportunity to play this game, baby. You better drop the hammer and get after this thing and have no regrets. And go to work on yourself with those five goals for 25 school days, 10 weekend days. That's exactly five weeks. Why do we go five weeks? Because it takes 21-28 days of committed, focused work to change your habits. When you change your habits, you change your life. So successful habits lead to successful softball players and people.

Make sure you surround yourself with like-minded people. If you're surrounded with people who are not committed to excellence, you'll get sucked down because you become the average of the five people you hang out with most.

And I want to hang out with you at least once a week and get a little bit of space in that mind of yours. So please listen to this audio. Please visit briancain.com/monday to sign up for my weekly message. And congratulations! You're now a master of the mental game. I am so proud of you for making it all the way through this audio. Please Tweet at me @briancainpeak with what you thought was the most powerful mental conditioning concept you learned through this whole 4RIP3 softball process.

I can't wait to see you dog-piling somewhere, someplace in this country when you win that championship because to win a championship, you've got to become a champion. And by going through this program, you, my friend, are well, well on your way to becoming a champion. Thank you. And Dominate the Day.

The Compound Effect
Tying It All Together
& Getting to Work

REVIEW SHEET

1. You grow most by doing a little a lot, not a lot a little. Mental toughness is like a muscle and it must be worked if it will grow. Just like a penny doubled a day will grow to over $10,000,000 in a month, your mental game will compound and your performance will grow with the daily investment and watering of the bamboo.

2. The challenge here is for you to listen to this 4RIP3 series of audios on a consistent basis. Every time you listen to them you are at a different place and will be a different person. As you grow and mature, you will get more out of listening to these audios. This is not the end; this is the beginning of you becoming the best you that you can possibly be.

3. Don't make the mistake that Cam made. You must use the program; it is not enough just to have it. If you don't use it, you will lose it. The program will only work if you work it.

4. It is the _____ that _____ most people.

5. Mental toughness _____ and helps you to be at your _____ when it means the _____.

6. The game _____ and the game is bigger than us all.

7. Have a big reason ____ and you will find a way ____.

8. Three steps to performance improvement taught to Cain by Harvey Dorfman:

   (1) A_____

1-10 How would you grade yourself?

(2) S_____

Start: _____

Stop: _____

Continue: _____

(3) A_____

9. The goal of the 4RIP3 System is to help you play one _____.

10. Know that the _____ is more important than the end result.

11. Your goal must be in your _____. You have control of the process, not the outcome.

12. Mentally tough athletes focus on what they _____ to do, not what they want to avoid.

13. The best team never wins; _____.

14. Practice makes _____ and changes softball practice into softball _____.

15. Four Stages of Commitment:

(1) J____ (2) W____ (3) C_____ (4) M_____

16. Have a mission for each day (goal) and a purpose (plan) for each day.

17. When you have _____ practice and step up every day, there is no step-up.

18. The key to learning is to totally immerse yourself and do a little _____, not a lot _____.

19. Read or listen to Cain's (1) *Daily Dominator message, (2) Monday e-mail, (3) these audios*

20. Four Stages of Acceptance:

    (1) This Ain't for Me

    (2) Ok for Others

    (3) I'll Try It

    (4) I Can't Believe I Did It Any Other Way

21. Three Steps to Memorizing Anything:

    (1) Location

    (2) Picture

    (3) Meaning

22. Cain's 4_ _ _ 3 System for Training Mental Toughness in Softball

R1 = R_____   I = M_____

R2 = R_____   P1 = P_____

R3 = R_____   P2 = P_____

R4 = R_____   P3 = P_____

23. The Right-hand Skeleton Files

    Location   Picture Meaning

(1) Head

You living inside a present & breathing

Live in the present moment by breathing

(2) Nose

Staircase, PRO athlete, one step/ball

Stick with the process of one step/pitch at a time

(3) Mouth

Remote control shaped as an ape

Control what you can control

(4) Ribs

Plus sign with words in, above and below

Positive, have to-want to, yet, compared to what

(5) Abs

A highlight video of you playing softball

Use mental imagery

(6) Hips

Hourglass

Routines

(7) Knees

Car wreck under signal lights

Recognize your signal lights

(8) Shins

Tattooed in RED; it says RELEASE / Toilet

Release the last pitch - flush it

(9) Feet

Camera on left foot to refocus; right = next pitch

Get green and refocus on the next pitch

(10) Ground

Domino's Pizza box that you smash

Dominate the Day

24. When is the most important day of your softball career? T_____ is the most important day.

25. Don't count the days... M_____.

26. Today + Today + T_____ = Your S_____ and your C_____.

27. The time is _____ and the place is _____.

28. Your bank account credits you with how much money every morning? $_____

29. The question I will ask you the most when I show up at practice is what are you _____?

30. Setting pre-practice goals helps you to get into the _____ moment for that day and that training session.

31. There are three major exercises that we do on a routine basis that help you to train your present-moment focus:

(1) Concentration grids

(2) 5-4-3-2-1 Relaxation and focus exercise

(3) Inhale & exhale 6-8 / 8-10 exercise

32. By using the _____ you can train yourself to focus for a longer period of time and recognize when your mind wanders out of the present moment.

33. Be sure to keep track of your concentration grid times because measurement equals _____.

34. You are training your relaxation response when you do breathing exercises. If you want to relax and get present 3-2 bases loaded, you must start training this response off the field.

35. The process is about giving yourself the best chance for s_____.

36. The process is about controlling what you can _____.

37. Your goal must be in your _____.

38. The process is about identifying the steps you must take to get to where you want to be.

39. The process is about competing with yourself and the _____, never the opponent.

40. The law of averages and the process say that four things can happen when you play softball:

    (1) Play well and win

    (2) Play well and lose

    (3) Play lousy and win

    (4) Play lousy and lose

41. There are seven ways to beat the game and give yourself the best chance for success. We call these process-based win indicators. They are part of the process of playing championship softball; and if you execute them, you give yourself the best chance for success.

42. We will memorize these using the Location/Picture/Meaning technique on the left hand.

    0 = Make no errors

    1 = Score first

    2 = Execute 2 out of 3 pitches for a strike

    3 = Hold opponent to 3 runs or less

    4 = Have 54% quality at-bats

    5 = Score 5 runs or more

    W = Win the freebie (free base) war

43. Your job as a hitter is to have a _____.

44. Your job as a pitcher is to throw _____.

45. Winning softball games is a _____ of working the process.

46. The way you stand for the N_____ is a part of the process.

47. How organized your locker is and how you manage your time are parts of the process.

48. You have two critical lists - your lists of what you CAN and CANNOT control.

49. Positive thinking is turning your have-to's into _____.

50. Positive thinking is focusing on what you _____ not what you are trying to avoid.

51. Positive thinking is knowing that you can do it - you just might not have done it _____.

52. Positive people have an attitude of _____ and you can build this by having a gratitude journal.

53. Positive people also know that others have it worse. They never make excuses and use the _____ mentality to give themselves the best peak performance state possible.

54. You should build your attitude of gratitude and positive perspective by creating a perspective poster.

55. The voice inside of your head that either is helping you to succeed or is killing your performance is called the voice of _____.

56. Confidence conditioning statements written down and reviewed on a routine basis will serve as the foundation for creating positive self-talk.

57. E + R = O stands for _____ = outcome. Positive people choose their responses.

58. Positive people know that will beats _____ in softball and the best team never wins.

59. Remember Roger Bannister? What was his significance on softball? There are no physical barriers, just mental barriers to overcome.

60. Creating a confidence resume is a great way to remind yourself of why you deserve to have success and why you are a good softball player. We all forget our previous wins and successes because we focus so much on what's happening in the future that we forget about our successful past. We must review our past to help us create the future we desire.

61. Get Big and fake it till you make it. Positive people know the BIG ABC's – A_____ big, B_____ big and C_____ big.

62. Mental imagery is also known as visualization and mental rehearsal. You do this without even knowing you do it.

63. Watching highlight videos of yourself or others playing the way you want to play is a great way to help you have positive mental images that you can refer back to when doing your imagery.

64. Doing r_____ before you do imagery is a good idea because when you are relaxed it sets the stage for more clear and vivid images.

65. When doing imagery, you want to use as many of your senses as possible.

66. Mental imagery is different than thinking about playing softball.

67. M_____ control leads to b_____ control leads to s_____ control.

68. Mental imagery is effective because the brain processes information, whether you vividly imagine it or physically do it, in similar psycho-neuromuscular pathways.

69. There are four steps to effective mental imagery:

   (1) Relaxation

   (2) Confidence Conditioning

   (3) Mental Recall

   (4) Mental Rehearsal

70. Softball hitters should do some good mental imagery when they are _____ hitters away.

71. Pitchers should do mental imagery as a part of their pre-pitch routine to help their body commit to the pitch that they want to execute/throw.

72. When doing imagery, you want to do a little a lot, not a lot a little. The more consistent you are, the better off you will be.

73. You should do mental imagery as a part of your pre-game and pre-pitch routine and use the attached audio the night before you compete.

74. The secrets of success are hidden in the routines of our daily lives.

75. Routines allow you to become more comfortable with what you are doing, which leads to confidence, which leads to consistency, which leads to your best chance for success.

76. The best players have pre-game and pre-practice routines that are similar so that you can approach each the same way, because your opponents are yourself and the game.

77. They also have pre-pitch routines that let us play pitch to pitch.

78. When we talk about routines, we want to use the image of an hourglass so that we have a definite start and end time for each pitch, inning, at-bat, practice and game.

79. When does an at-bat start? When you put your _____ or helmet on. When is an at-bat over? When you take the gloves or helmet off.

80. Inside of your routine you want to have a place where you take a deep _____ on a focal _____, have a final _____ and a r_____ so that you can stay consistent in your approach.

81. If you are not in the line-up, you want to take _____ reps with the person who is playing your position.

82. Be sure that you visit www.briancain.com/softball to watch the routine videos that are available so you can see top college softball players and ESPN announcers talking about the at-bat and pitching routines.

83. The ability to recognize where you are mentally, physically and emotionally when competing is also known as having awareness and being able to recognize your _____.

84. What you are _____ of you can control; what you are _____ of will control you.

85. What are some ways that you recognize when you are confident and in green lights? How do you recognize when you start to lose it and get into yellow and then beat yourself by playing in red lights?

86. Green   Yellow Red

    A = Self-talk

    B = Physical Feelings

    C = Situations

87. When you struggle in softball, you will often become one of three players:

    (1) Primal

    (2) Prayer

    (3) Perfect

88. The term "check in" refers to your checking in on your signal lights and getting a good breath, but also on shifting your attention from what if (results) to what is (process) and onto what is important now. A good time for a coach or teammate to say "check in" would be when he or she sees something happen that could trigger yellow or red lights or cause you to focus on the wrong thing. Use the term "check in" to remind a teammate to get back to green after something outside of your _____ happens.

89. Inside of your routine, when you recognize that you are in a yellow or red light, you must have a pre-determined physical release that you go to that helps you to mentally release the last pitch and refocus back to what's important now. What's important now is always the next pitch.

4RIP3 Softball Mental Conditioning Program

90. We used the verbal "C_____ I___" for recognize; you must now think "S__ W____" as your release and "Next Pitch" as your refocus cue. The term "So What, Next Pitch" really means release and refocus.

91. What are some physical ways that you can release a yellow or red light and get back to a green?

(1) Finding a focal point and taking a deep breath.

(2) Undoing your batting gloves and restrapping them to refocus you to the next pitch and get a deep breath.

(3) Wiping the pitcher's rubber as a way to wipe away the last pitch.

(4) Taking off your glove and smoothing out the dirt in the infield or the grass, and then taking a deep breath and putting your glove back on to get to the next pitch.

92. Using your post-practice routine is a great way to release at the end of practice. It will help you leave softball at softball, to be able to walk away and leave the _____ from the day behind you and to focus on what you need to do as a student.

93. Being able to see coaching and constructive criticism as a compliment vs. an attack is an example of being able to separate softball from who you are to _____.

94. Being able to separate from professional vs. _____ will help you a LOT when you get into a professional career. It will enable you to grow and take constructive criticism to get better vs. take it as an attack and get bitter.

95. When you recognize that you are in green lights, you should go right to refocusing on the next pitch. Refocusing means that you come up with a plan for the next pitch.

96. When you recognize that you are in red or yellow lights and are carrying the metaphorical mental brick that will weigh you down if you carry it for more than a few seconds, you must be able to release that brick and get to the next pitch.

97. If you recognize that you have yellow or red lights, you have to _____ before you play the next pitch. There are many things you can do as a release; the biggest one for softball is taking a releasing deep breath before you take your refocusing deep breath on your focal point to lock into the next pitch.

98. If you want more, you must become more.

99. Set five personal development plan goals, then put them on your right hand and memorize them just like you did the 7 ways to beat the game when competing against yourself and the game.

100. Keep these five personal development plan goals for a total of five weeks so that you get 25 school days and 10 weekend days. It takes 21-28 days of commitment and focused work to change your habits. After five weeks, re-evaluate where you are with your personal development plan goals and get back to work on yourself with a new set, or keep the ones that you feel still need your attention.

101. Be sure that you surround yourself with like-minded players and people who are committed to excellence, as you will become the average of the _____ people you hang out with most.

SAMPLE CHAPTER FROM CAIN'S BOOK

CHAMPIONS TELL ALL

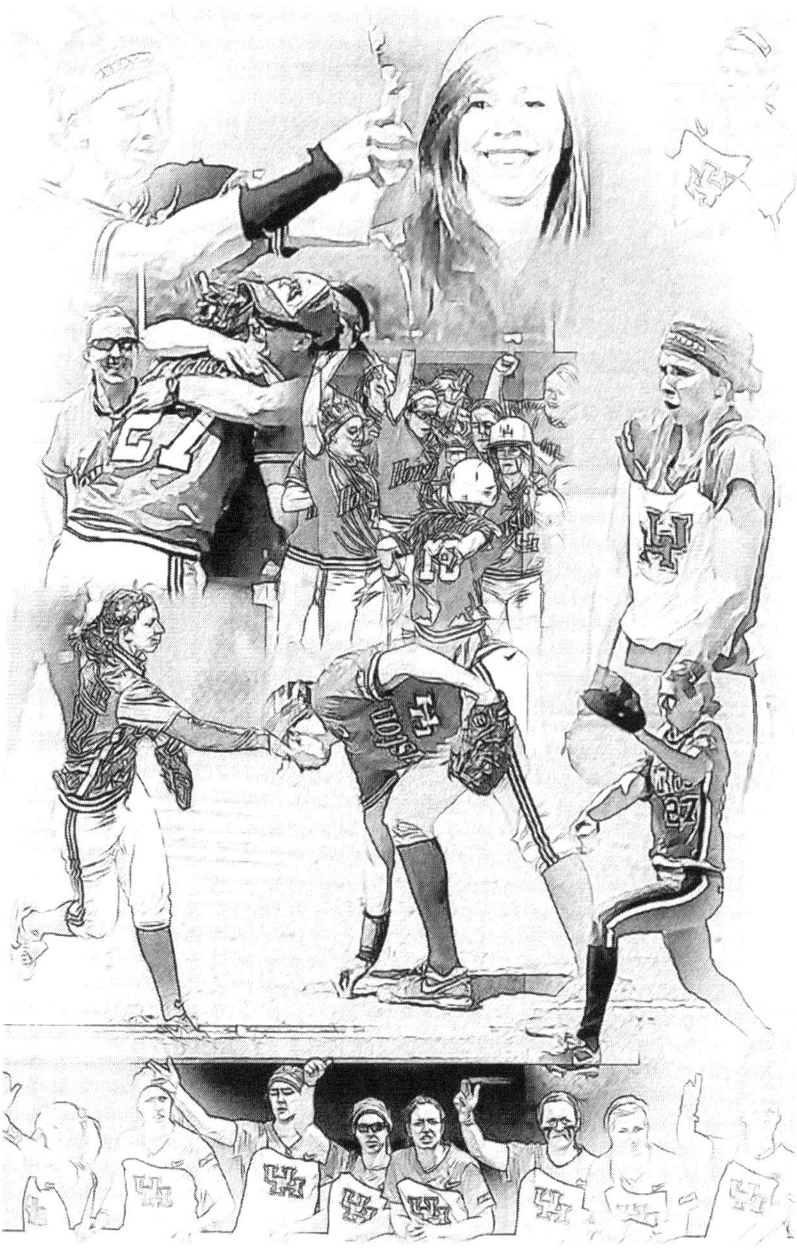

SAMPLE CHAPTER

AMANDA CRABTREE, SOFTBALL PITCHER USES MENTAL GAME TO TURN CAREER AROUND & LEADS COUNTRY IN STRIKEOUTS PER GAME

Amanda Crabtree was one of the top pitchers in all of college softball during the 2011 season. She led the country in strikeouts per seven innings and led her team to one game from the NCAA Women's College World Series and to one of the best seasons in history at The University of Houston. She discusses how the mental game made a difference for her on and off the diamond and was the missing piece of her performance puzzle.

Crabtree grew up in Kingwood, Texas, and went to Kingwood High School where she played all four years on the school's varsity softball team. She also played on a top select team out of Houston as well as participated in high school volleyball her freshman year.

WHEN TO FOCUS ON ONE SPORT

I knew that softball was my sport and would be the sport that I could play in college so I started focusing on just playing softball after my freshman year of high school because that specialization would give me the best chance to play in college. I started getting recruited at the end of my freshman year and started getting contacted by college coaches through emails to my coaches.

FINDING THE COLLEGE OF YOUR CHOICE

I decided to go to Oklahoma State. My parents were really supportive of whatever I wanted do and that was the best thing that I think parents can do, support the decision that your son or daughter makes in where they want to pursue their college education. There were definitely some things that I was looking for in schools.

Going into college athletics from high school, you do not always know what you are getting yourself into and I am not sure you can ever be totally prepared for the jump from high school to college in any sport. All you can do is make the best decision based on all the information you have at the time, trust your gut and go with it. I chose Oklahoma State. I loved Stillwater, Oklahoma where the school is and I loved the traditions. I loved everything about the school and the program.

COLLEGE SPORTS CAN BE A RUDE AWAKENING

When I got to Oklahoma State for my freshman year, things did not go as expected. It was a lot harder for me to be away from home than I had expected. I was dealing with injuries for the first time in my career and that was a major stressor for me. Freshman year was a big wakeup call. I give pitching lessons now, and I always tell my students that college softball is a lot different than what you think of high school softball and even competitive travel softball. It's a huge step up in competition and I do not think my mind was prepared for that level of softball.

FAILS FOR FIRST TIME

It was the first time that I had faced a lot of adversity and I was not prepared to deal with it. I had not developed the skill set yet to embrace adversity and did not see adversity as a part of the growth process that is necessary and required to take your game to the next level. I saw myself as a failure.

It was really, really tough on me. I had a lot of doubts about myself and my talent. I struggled a lot with whether or not I should even keep playing. My parents and I had a lot of late night phone calls and discussions about my future in softball.

I had lost my love for the game and figured I needed to try to find a place to play closer to home. So, I was back at "square one" being recruited again and ended up at The University of Houston, who had recruited me out of high school.

FRESH START, SAME CHALLENGES

I was excited for a fresh start. I transferred my sophomore year and it felt like my freshman year all over. I was brand new to the program, did not know anyone and felt like I was still falling short of my potential. I was expecting everything to change and nothing changed for me. I started to doubt myself again. I was putting in all the work, working as hard as I possibly could, maybe too hard at times and just was not getting the results that I felt I should be getting. My sophomore year was pretty miserable.

ANOTHER YEAR, ANOTHER STRUGGLE

Junior year got a little bit better but I didn't really meet any of the goals I set for myself. I lost my confidence and my focus on the process in games most of the time and kept getting disappointed with myself. I was thinking about quitting; the game was just not fun for me anymore.

KEY TO UNLOCKING POTENTIAL IS FOUND

When my senior year came along our coach, Kyla Holas, had a mental conditioning coach, Brian Cain, come and work with our team and staff. The three days we spent together as a team were eye opening for me. I think it was a combination of Coach Holas teaching me about the process and the way that Cain conveyed some of the same concepts, but it just started to make sense to me.

UNIQUE STYLE – FINDING OUT WHO YOU NEED TO BE

I always thought I was supposed to be a the stoic, unemotional pitcher who was ultra-aggressive and might even cursing at a batter and be fired up with competitiveness to beat you. I tried to make myself that pitcher and it did not work for me. I am a very realistic person who is comfortable in my own skin and just being me. I pitch with my emotions on my sleeve, and those emotions are usually a big smile or laugh because I love playing softball and don't feel like I need to get fired up or make it personal between me and the hitter. I had always thought that my true personality was a weakness of mine in competition and never really had people who embraced that style around me, but once I learned I could just be me, I had a lot more success.

AH HA MOMENT

I remember having a conversation one day with Cain when I asked, "Do you think that it's weird that when I get kind of stressed out during a game I stop and pray?"

Then Cain said, "You know, you are not the only pitcher that does that. There are closers in Major League Baseball that will go out to the mound and know that the result is out of their control. They say it is in God's hands and that they just execute a pitch and let the outcome take care of itself. Whatever works for you, works for you."

And from that moment on a light bulb went off and I realized that what I had been doing, trying to be a pitcher that showed no emotion and was stoic and tough was just not who I needed to be to have success.

I had been trying to fit this mold of somebody else, and it made me miserable. I started to do the things that I used to do and made the game fun again. Next thing you know, I was getting the results I always wanted and having a lot more fun in the process.

It was a big transition in the way that I thought, the way that I performed and the way that I practiced. I was having so much fun just playing the game of softball as if it was a game and not life and death. I realized that my self-worth was not tied up in how well I pitched, but that I was two separate people. Who I was as an athlete and who I was as a person. Softball was not who I was, it was what I did, and that approach made the game a lot more fun and turned all the pressure I had felt into pleasure.

REGRETS & EXPENSIVE EXPERIENCE

It makes me so sad, sometimes, that it took me three years of being miserable to figure out that I should not be treating the game like it was life and death, *that I needed to have fun to play well and not just have fun when I played well*.

TALENT IS OVERRATED

I went from being a pitcher who struggled for three years to leading the country in strikeouts per seven innings pitched and was in the top two or three pitchers in the country in hits given up per seven innings. I felt like I was finally having the success I had worked so hard for and the success that my ability and the quality of the coaching I had received should have allowed me to have.

Physical talent is never enough. You can have tremendous physical talent, but if you don't think the right way or you're not having fun and you're putting more pressure than you need to on yourself to be perfect, you're not going to have success.

I had all of the tools. I always tell people that I was no better as a pitcher in my senior year of college than I was my first three. I simply got my head screwed on straight. Literally, my pitches did not get any better. I didn't suddenly develop three new pitches that were fantastic or out of this world. I had the same pitches that were good every other year, but all of a sudden I learned to control the six inches between my ears where it used to control me.

ANALYSIS PARALYSIS

I am a very big analyzer. I analyze everything to death, which is a good trait to have as a pitcher, if you can keep it under control. I analyze to paralysis.

I used to get scouting reports and it would paralyze me because I would be thinking so much about the report and who was on deck and what I was supposed to throw that I could not keep my focus in the moment and on playing this pitch, and to be successful in softball you must go one pitch at a time.

PERFECTIONISM KILLS PERFORMANCE

I was a perfectionist. I had to be perfect no matter what and so I became a checklist pitcher. I always had a checklist that I had to do for each pitch and I let that over-analysis, in an attempt to be perfect in an imperfect game, affect my pace.

When I was stressed out or when I was mad at myself, I would not breathe and refocus between pitches. I didn't ever take time to check in on my signal lights or my breathing; I just got the ball and started thinking. All of that thinking really slowed down my pace and zapped me of my confidence and belief.

ROUTINE HELPS SET PACE

I really had no mental game routine. I tried to repeat my mechanics physically, but always rushed physically because I was rushing mentally. I was playing three, four, sometimes five pitches ahead instead of going one pitch at a time.

I really worked on a routine and my breathing each pitch in the fall before my senior year and I think that was a big game changer for me. The people who played against me my senior year really hated hitting off me because I took my time and had a slower pace than most pitchers, but it was the exact pace I needed to pitch my best.

I always tried to have a fast pace and should have worked to find the right pace. The pace of my new, slower routine worked for me. I took my time. I would always go to the back of the mound and visualize the last pitch I threw, but it going exactly where I wanted it to go. I always took a huge breath and just let all of the stress that I would put on myself go.

CHANGE SELF TALK, CHANGE YOUR LIFE

The main thing that changed for me was the way that I talked to myself. I used to analyze everything to death. Even a good pitch, I would find something wrong with it. When I finally realized that as a pitcher you have the odds in your favor, and all you need to do is just make quality pitches, my whole game changed.

I learned that no pitcher is perfect. Sometimes, you throw flat rise balls, you throw curve balls that hang. I would just say, "OK. That pitch is gone, nothing I can do about it now, let's just move on with the next one." Prior to my senior year, I would've been very disappointed in myself. And I would've had so much stress on me that the negative spiral would have continued. I would have taken that yellow light of a poor pitch and it would have immediately snowballed into a red light.

GREEN SHOELACES

As the game went on, normally, the stress got greater and greater for me. Before my senior year, I never had a way to let the stress go personally, and neither did we as a team.

One of the ways our team helped each other get to the next pitch was to have everyone wear one green shoelace. The green shoelace was important because when the game started to speed up on me, and I was not performing well, like most athletes, one of the first things that would happen was that my head would go down. Now when my head went down, I would see the green shoelace and it reminded me to get to the next pitch.

USE THE SHOELACE AS A RELEASE

When the game sped up on me and I needed to stop and slow it down, I would step out of the circle, call time out and retie my shoe. This physical pause would help me to take a mental pause and I felt like it removed me from the situation, allowed me to flush everything that had happened in the past, and get my mind and body back to where I needed to be in the present.

Sometimes, the other team would get frustrated and I am sure my teammates may have as well because I might tie my shoes as many as three times in an inning if I was struggling, and they knew that nothing was coming untied. However, that release of untying my shoes really helped me stay in a positive and green light mindset.

I think many athletes perform well when they are talking negative to themselves. One of my biggest challenges was always quieting the voice of negativity that would show up in competition. I needed to have a physical release to stop and reset myself when I started to spiral out of control.

SENIOR YEAR = TOTALLY DIFFERENT PITCHER

I was a totally different pitcher my senior year and I think it was largely due to me changing everything except for my pitching. I changed my routine. I changed my self-talk. I changed how seriously I took myself, I changed almost everything mentally and hardly anything physically, if anything at all.

Before my senior year, if I pitched badly, I thought that I was a bad person. I didn't separate softball from real life. Softball was who I was, not what I did. When I started to separate who I was as a competitor and who I was as a person, it really wasn't such a big deal to have a bad day at the field anymore because I did not take it with me to my personal life, and this really helped me to minimize my poor performance streaks because every day was a new day versus everyday being life and death. I was able to have a bad day and say, "OK, let's move on, and let's do better the next time."

SEPARATING LIFE AS PERSON AND COMPETITOR

A big mistake that athletes make is they look at softball as who they are, not what they do. And they live and die with every pitch and live and die with every game. When you can separate yourself from the game and see yourself and your self-worth as a human being not tied up in your performance, you're going to perform better. A lot of players have a pre-practice routine they use to get locked into being a softball player and a post-practice they use to let go of being a softball player. I didn't necessarily have anything that you would've seen.

A lot of my teammates used the changing of their clothes as a way to help separate from softball to their real self. When the uniform was on, they were the softball player, when it was off they were the student. For me, it was more of a mental attitude shift when I put my cleats on, I put on my softball attitude. And then when I took them off, I put on my real-world attitude.

SOFTBALL IS NOT LIFE AND DEATH

I think that when most athletes are not happy with their performance on a consistent basis, this happens because they are living and dying by their successes on the field. I can personally say that I lived my first three years of college determining my self-worth by how my softball went.

A lot of athletes make the mistake of personalizing performance and seeing their self-worth wrapped up in how they perform in sport. It happens a lot I think because as a college athlete, you put so much of yourself into your sport and into what you do that you take that success and failure very personal. As with a lot of things we've talked about, personalizing performance can be good and bad. There's nothing in life that's good or bad. It's always good *and* bad. And personalizing that performance is good in the sense that it's going to motivate you to work harder and to do better. However, when you get to a certain level of competition, for me it was college softball, being the perfectionist and personalizing performance zaps you of any confidence that you might have because you are going to struggle, at some point, when you play against the best players in the country. If you are a perfectionist or evaluate as good or bad and fail to accept that you should evaluate as good *and* bad, you end up beating yourself.

CAIN'S COACHING POINT:
Being a perfectionist is both good and **bad. How is being a perfectionist both good and bad for you?**

_____

_____

_____

THE PERFECTIONIST TEST

My senior year we won the NCAA Regional at The University of Texas and went to Oklahoma State for the NCAA Super Regional. Coach Holas noticed that we were tight before the game and had us all step inside of a bucket with water to prove that we could not walk on water. Her point was taken and we loosened up immediately.

When you are putting in 20-40 hours a week practicing, it feels like you should be perfect. And having us try to walk on water, as elementary as it sounds, was a great way to reinforce this point rather than just talking about it.

Every single person is going to make mistakes throughout this journey, and that's ok, it is all about how you respond to those mistakes that defines who you are and who you become. Prior to walking on water, I think everybody was tense. It was a big game. It was the second time the University of Houston had ever been to super-regionals and her test to walk on water really helped to settle our nerves and refocused us on playing our game and playing pitch to pitch.

FOCAL POINTS HELP TO REFOCUS

When I would get stressed, an umpire would miss a call, a teammate would make an error or if I was doubting myself or not having the positive self-talk, those little things used to be big things to me. Finding a focal point was a critical part of my being able to release those negatives and refocus on going one pitch at a time.

During the game I would turn around and focus on a needle on the top of a building in deep center field. That needle was my focal point and the place I looked when I needed to release my red lights and get back into green.

That needle worked better for me as a focal point than the second base bag or a foul pole would have. I liked it because it was far away from softball. I was looking at downtown Houston, of all these massive buildings made of glass and metal, and I was playing on this great manicured dirt and grass. It was a polar opposite and gave me that, "OK. This is just a game. There's more to life, this is not life" feeling and it would ground me.

I would look at my focal point, wipe the chalk off the back of the pitchers circle and say, "OK. It's done. I'm moving on. Next

Pitch!" I always thought that when I turned around and faced the batter again that it was done. It was in the past, there was nothing I could do about it anymore. All I could do was pitch the next pitch.

This release and the focal point gave me a systematic way to constantly release the little things that irritate you over the course of a game and can go from being a small nag into a big problem if you let them.

If I didn't agree with the umpire's call or if I was in red lights, I would go to my focal point and release. If I was having a bad game, I might do this a hundred times that game. Most games, I may have only looked at it twice. My focal point gave me a way where people didn't really know what I was doing, to give me peace of mind and get me back in that green light mentality, and it really helped. The release and the focal point gave me a way to stop and slow down rather than trying to work faster, which is what a lot of people do and that never helped me, and I don't think helps very many people.

SPORT SPECIALIZATION

Recruiting for college athletics has gone from finding the best juniors and seniors in high school to the best seventh and eighth graders in the country. Even though this is the case for the best 1% of players in the country, I always encourage young people to play just about every sport under the sun growing up. I swam for a long time and played softball, soccer, volleyball, basketball, and also ran track and danced.

I knew that when I chose softball, it was the one sport that I really wanted to choose. I think some athletes that specialize in one sport quit other sports too soon and always wonder if they had just played a little longer, what would have happened?

My advice to younger athletes is to always try as many sports as you can because you may think that you like one sport and you're going to try another sport, and you might like it better.

There may come a time where you realize that you love one sport and are just going to play that sport. I kind of whittled my sports down until I really knew, confidently, that softball was what I wanted to put all of my time and effort into. When you're starting to get recruited by colleges, you're going to have to make up your mind because I think if you want to do yourself justice and find the best fit for yourself, you do have to specialize in one sport, especially if you're a pitcher. I think if you play other positions you have a little bit more flexibility. But softball pitching is so demanding that I think you have to choose early or you will be behind the competition.

That was the challenge I was faced with. I couldn't play club volleyball, high school volleyball, travel softball and high school softball and be good at them all. That is what I wanted, to do them all, but I had to make a choice.

DO YOU PICK SPORT, OR DOES SPORT PICK YOU?

Sometimes you get to pick when you want to specialize and other times, the sport kind of makes that choice for you. It may depend on where you live and how competitive the sports are in your area or it may depend on what sport you want to play at the next level.

Sometimes, your sport's going to dictate that you commit full-time, but if you are young, my message is get involved early in as many sports as you can and then stay involved in the ones that you love until it's time, if you want to play in college, for you to specialize. If you don't want to play in college, then maybe you don't need to specialize.

MENTAL IMAGERY PLAYS LARGE ROLE IN PREPARATION

I always struggled with self-confidence, especially after the first three years that I had. I had a lot of self-doubt. I had never struggled in softball until I got to college, so failure was something that I just didn't really know how to deal with.

My senior year, I dedicated myself to using mental imagery as a part of my preparation routine. I would sit down when there were two outs, find a spot on the bench by myself, close my eyes, and go through the warm-ups that I was about to go and throw on the mound.

Every inning, I had the same warm-up routine.

1. Curve out
2. Curve in
3. Rise
4. Drop out
5. Screw
6. Curve out

I would visualize myself throwing the most amazing curve ball, outside, I'd ever thrown. I'd go through all the pitches I was going to throw in my warm ups and I would throw them the best I had ever thrown them. Then, when I walked out onto the mound, I already had six awesome pitches under my belt. And then all those pitches in warm-ups just built on top of each other and my confidence would grow from there.

It was a really good way for me to stay in touch with the game. Pitchers can sometimes get lethargic in the dugout, especially during a long inning, and your mind can start to kind of wander. Using mental imagery in the dugout was a really good way for me not to lose anything. It was a way for me to see good pitches in my mind, feel them in my body and I didn't have to tire my arms or my body out by throwing them.

Doing mental imagery of those warm up pitches was an important part of my routine that got me mentally ready for the inning that was I going into, but it also gave me that little boost of confidence. Even though I didn't throw a pitch, I walked out there feeling like all my pitches were on.

RECOGNIZING YOUR SIGNAL LIGHTS

I think one of the biggest challenges athletes have is recognizing when they're out of that green light mentality and are getting into yellow or red so they can recognize they are starting to lose it so they can change their thought process, stop the bleeding, and turn it around, one pitch at a time.

Recognizing my signal lights was something that was a challenge for me at first. I worked on recognizing my signal lights with my pitching coach Abbie Simms a lot that fall. She was really good at being like, "OK, Amanda, you're getting a little bit crazy right now, step off and release." She would just say enough where I would be like, "Oh, you're right. I'm kind of rushing right now. I'm not doing a very good job of going pitch to pitch." She started pointing out some things and then it made me more aware.

AWARENESS IS THE FIRST STEP TO ACCOMPLISHMENT

I became so in tune with the way that my body worked that whenever I was feeling stressed, I literally could feel the heat drive through my body. It was crazy. It was like I could feel my blood boiling when I got into red lights and it allowed me to recognize, release and refocus on the next pitch.

When my mind was good and I was in green lights, my thoughts were slow and clear. When I would get frustrated or things were starting to spin out of control, my thoughts would start to race.

CAIN'S COACHING POINT:
Start to gain an awareness of when you perform at your best and when you perform at your worst so that you can better recognize when you are beating yourself and turn it around by changing your self-talk, releasing your negative thoughts and getting back into the present moment.

WHEN AT MY BEST (GREEN) I WOULD DESCRIBE MY:

THOUGHTS/SELF-TALK:

_____

_____

_____

PHYSICAL FEELINGS:

_____

_____

WHEN AT MY WORST (RED) I WOULD DESCRIBE MY:

THOUGHTS/SELF-TALK:

_____

_____

_____

PHYSICAL FEELINGS:

_____

_____

Becoming aware of my thoughts and feelings took a lot of practice. Every day, I had to check in on my thoughts and feelings when I was pitching. It also helped that I really trusted Abbie and I knew she wasn't just going to say, "Hey, Amanda. You're getting crazy," when I wasn't. She wanted me to figure it out on my own and asked me a lot of questions, which helped to build my self-awareness.

Finding somebody that you can trust and who can see you when you start to get into red lights is key. Our third baseman would sometimes come over and just talk to me for a second because she could tell that I was just a little bit out of my rhythm and it would slow me back down and help me get back into the rhythm I needed to pitch my best.

I think if you really work together as a team, you start to learn when people are totally out of whack. And if they're not realizing, there's somebody on the team that can go up and be like, "Hey. You need to tie your shoe" and it will be ok because that relationship has been established and you trust their words.

SO WHAT NEXT PITCH MENTALITY

I was a big over-thinker; I am a big planner. In softball though, you can't plan anything other than the pitch you are about to throw. I used to think about what I was going to do 3, 4, 5 pitches from now and I would get so far away from the present moment and this pitch that I beat myself.

There would be times my first three years where if they got a runner on base I would be thinking, "Oh my gosh. If this next person gets on and then I walk the next person, the bases are going to be loaded and then I'm going to give up a grand slam."

That's how I would think. Once I learned the "so what, next pitch" mentality and started to really understand what it meant to play one pitch at a time, all of sudden, pitching and handling the stress that comes with pitching was much easier.

It was so much easier to let all those things go. It was so much easier to think about the game because all you were thinking about was one thing at a time. Again, it takes a lot of time and team building to get there, but once you know each other, it becomes a part of your culture and part of how you talk with each other. "So what, next pitch" is all you can say at certain times. "So what" means you acknowledge that the result was not what you wanted and that there is NOTHING you can do at this present moment about the past. "Next pitch" gives you the right thing to focus on, playing and winning the next pitch.

MENTAL GAME EXTENDS INTO LIFE AFTER SOFTBALL

Everything that I have learned in the mental game of softball I still use every day in my life after softball. I am a kindergarten teacher and use the skills I learned through the mental game of softball in my life every day. I teach my five-year-old kindergartners how to use the same skills every single day. Skills like not counting the days, but making the days count have been huge for me as a teacher.

ANTIDOTE FOR THE GRIND OF EVERYDAY WORK

I, like most people, get in the mindset where you're working and it's like, "Oh, another day at work. Oh, another day at work. Oh, another day at work." and you kind of lose that wow factor and the excitement that you had when you first got hired.

Especially being a teacher, you can lose the awe of being a teacher. I wanted to be a teacher for the longest time. I think it's the absolute coolest job there is and you put so much of yourself into what you do that there are times where you get really tired. You're worn down. Having the mental skills like a "compared to what" perspective or to recognize when you are in red lights versus green lights and having routines helps you to bring the energy and commitment to excellence that you need to bring everyday and that your students deserve.

DOMINATE THE DAY

I wake up every day with the goal to dominate the day. I try to make every day the best day I have ever had in the classroom. Teaching kids can be exhausting. It can be a handful, especially when they don't listen, which is most of the time.

Having releases and a way to let go of the negative emotion and frustration has been huge. I may get frustrated during the day, but I can't show them I'm frustrated. So I have to come up with a way to let those emotions go because it's not a five-year-old's fault. Just like it's not softball's fault.

I think the way that I learned to deal with the stress and pressure of softball prepared me better than anything else for real life: a career. Stopping to take a breath has been one of the most beneficial skills I have taken from softball to the classroom.

SPORT DOES NOT DEFINE YOU

Softball does not define you as a person because the moment that you really understand that you are not your performance, everything that you do is going to get better. No one thing in your life defines you. I think that too many people and too many athletes don't realize that your career or your sport does not define who you really are. I wish I had learned that a lot earlier in my career.

You can contact Amanda Crabtree by email at abcrabtree27@yahoo.com.

AMANDA CRABTREE REVIEW

- [ ] When to focus on one sport
- [ ] Finding the college of your choice
- [ ] College sports can be a rude awakening
- [ ] Fails for first time
- [ ] Fresh start, same challenges
- [ ] Another year, another struggle
- [ ] Key to unlocking potential is found
- [ ] Unique style – finding out who you need to be
- [ ] Ah ha moment
- [ ] Regrets & expensive experience
- [ ] Talent is overrated
- [ ] Analysis paralysis
- [ ] Perfectionism kills performance
- [ ] Routine helps set pace
- [ ] Change self-talk, change your life
- [ ] Green shoelaces
- [ ] Use the shoelace as a release
- [ ] Senior year = totally different pitcher
- [ ] Separating life as person and competitor
- [ ] Softball is not life and death
- [ ] The perfectionist test
- [ ] Focal points help to refocus
- [ ] Sport specialization
- [ ] Do you pick sport, or does sport pick you?

- [ ] **Mental imagery plays large role in preparation**
- [ ] **Recognizing your signal lights**
- [ ] **Awareness is the first step to accomplishment**
- [ ] **So what, next pitch mentality**
- [ ] **Mental game extends into life after softball**
- [ ] **Antidote for the grind of everyday work**
- [ ] **Dominate the day**
- [ ] **Sport does not define you**

SAMPLE CHAPTER FROM CAIN'S BOOK

SO WHAT, NEXT PITCH!

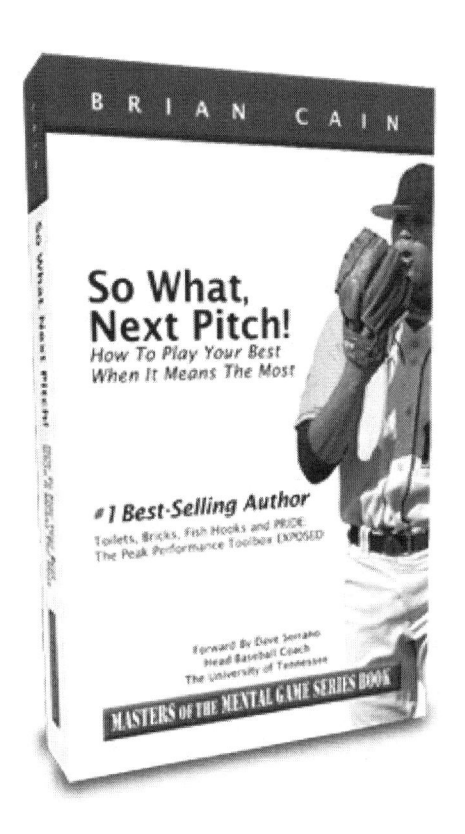

NATIONAL CHAMPIONSHIP MENTAL CONDITIONING
Alabama's Patrick Murphy

Shares Essentials of Tide's Mental-Conditioning Program

BC: Coach Murphy, you're one of the most successful softball coaches in the country and led The University of Alabama Softball Program to the 2012 NCAA National Championship. If I were to ask you to talk about mental conditioning for the game of softball, what sort of things would you talk about?

PM: Softball is definitely a mental game. If the athlete feels good about herself, it's definitely going to carry over into the softball performance side of it. If she's not feeling good about herself, it's definitely going to negatively affect her on the field as well. *I think the mental game is a huge part of our game with female athletes.*

BC: Are there things that you do as the coach to try to make the players feel good before the game?

PM: We talk about past performances or practices that week if somebody did really well or will look at pre-game batting practice. I've changed lineups ten minutes before the game, when somebody has had a great batting practice, and I'll go up to her individually and say, "You know, you deserve to start, you were awesome today."

More times than not they've rewarded us with great performances. Batting practice carries over to the game in softball a lot I think. Sometimes it's a gut feeling, but most of the time if they look good, you can tell that they feel good about where they are at that day and how they are playing, and then chances are they're going to play well in the game.

SIGNS OF SUCCESS

BC: If I were to ask about coaching the mental game, what are some of the things you would talk about? You have the "Process over Outcome" and "Get Big" signs in the dugout and the "Two Outs, So What?" sign on the foul pole. What are some of the things you do that you consider coaching the mental game?

PM: *The signs serve as great reminders for us, they're great visual cues of the thought processes that we want to have. We do a lot of daily reminders about the process*. I probably talk at least three times a practice about putting a good swing on the ball, and if the outfielder makes a diving catch, that's a great at-bat, it's a great swing, and take confidence from that. Feel good about it because you crushed it.

In the weight room, we talk about the mental game all the time. Conditioning is a chance to improve mental toughness and when you have a hard workout or a run and you might not feel like you want to do it, or you can't do it, that's a great time to practice your mental game and *act differently than how you feel*.

We're in the weight room three times a week all year so it's a great time to utilize the mental skills we want on the field. *Whenever I read anything about a similar situation of an athlete, I clip out the article and send it to whomever I think it mirrors on my team.*

SHARING OF ARTICLES A SUCCESS

BC: Can you think of one specific example that you've used with an article or share a story that you felt has made a difference?

PM: After the Texas Christian University team played so well in the baseball 2010 College World Series, I was researching them on the internet and there was an article about their captain and catcher, Bryan Holiday, that was all about his journey of becoming, behind the scenes, a starter and then all of a sudden he is the guy holding everybody accountable. It was perfect for one of our seniors this year.

Holiday talked about how he had to hold a teammate accountable and it was uncomfortable for him but he made the choice that he would rather win than not, and he would rather be respected than liked. I think that's a lot tougher for female athletes to do than male athletes because they're extremely worried about whether people like them.

BC: Some of the best leaders that you've had, have they fallen into that category of rather being respected than liked?

PM: Definitely. We had one in our first four years in the program. We had no business of playing in a regional final in our fourth year, and I think it was largely due to this one player. Christy Kyle was one of the best leaders we've ever had.

CHARACTERISTICS OF A GREAT LEADER

BC: What were some of the characteristics that made her a great leader?

PM: She was tougher on herself than anyone else. *She held herself to a higher standard of excellence*. She was one of the first players I had coached who walked the walked so she could talk the talk. She was not afraid to get into people's faces and it was very much her policing the team herself.

I can remember several articles written about Pat Summit and the University of Tennessee women's basketball program that said you know you have a successful program when the players themselves police their fellow teammates. When we started doing that I felt like we were going to be successful.

CORE COVENANTS ARE KEY

BC: Shift gears here a little bit and talk about the core covenants of Alabama Softball. You have had these as the foundation of your program for years. What is the purpose of your program's core covenants and what difference have they made in the program?

PM: *What our core covenants provide is a systematic way of saying, we want the whole package, we don't want just a winning softball team; we want good citizens, good students, good teammates, people who will give back to the community, and all the things that go into being a good human being.* That is how we want to do things and we want them to start living those values as early as possible.

We want them to realize that there's life after softball. That's one of the hardest things; unlike baseball, there are not many opportunities after college for playing the game, and we've got to get them prepared for that sudden moment when it's over.

A lot of our core covenants help them with getting out in the community and doing internships with their majors and realizing that every time they shake a hand it's a six-second job interview.

BC: So the core covenants really are not just going to help them win games in softball, but they're going to help them win in life?

PM: Definitely. I think the process opens their eyes a little bit; they know that this is a four-year gig, that's it. *It's our job as coaches to use these four years to prepare them for a long and successful life after softball*. Their four years at the University of Alabama go by extremely fast and we want to make sure they take advantage of all the opportunities presented to them. They need to realize that they're not going to be a celebrity for the rest of their life as they may be here for four years and there are a lot of things that go into preparing them for the real world, a lot of the things we talk about with the covenants and our mission statement.

FOUNDATIONS OF SUCCESS

BC: You've had a lot of success here at the University of Alabama: Southeastern Conference Championships, College World Series appearances. What would you say is the foundation of your program? If you had to say, "These are the things that have been consistent with every team we've had that has been successful," what would those things be?

PM: *When you surround yourself with good people, good things happen.* We have been blessed to have great assistant coaches, great athletic trainers, managers, strength coaches, and players. I can't think of a negative staff member whom we've had, and that's a rarity. I'm still great friends with one of our first athletic trainers and one of our first student-managers. There is a huge sense of family in our program.

We teach our players that we want people who want to be here. That's our #1 goal in recruiting. Once you're on campus as an Alabama softball player, there's no such thing as divorce in our program, you're here and you're going to be here for four or five years and we're going to figure out a way to make you successful. There are going to be ups and downs and we'll work through them, but once you're here you're stuck with us and we're stuck with you, so we have to commit to making it work.

We've only had one kid who played four years and didn't graduate. You're going to see your teammates more than your own family so we want to get along and definitely want to have fun with what we do.

BC: You said "surround yourself with good people," is there anything else that you feel has been a cornerstone of your success?

PM: I think *we still have an underdog mentality*. I always say we haven't done anything yet until we win a national championship, and we're still the underdog. We're still fighting for respect. Play with a chip on your shoulder. I think if they believe that they've arrived, that is when we will get humbled and are going to get passed by. I think when you consider yourself the underdog, you don't settle, you stay humble and hungry.

BC: Is there anything that I haven't asked you that you think is important, any last nuggets of wisdom?

PM: We had our staff meeting the other day and one of the first things they said is that *we want to look for new and different ways to teach the game. We want to be innovative. We want to be creative. We don't want to be the "same old, same old" again because if you stand still you're going to get passed*. So we're always looking for new and different ways to do things.

However, you must also continue to do the things that you have done that have made you successful. Don't forget those things. It's kind of like Vince Lombardi and the Green Bay Packers. They had five plays and they mastered those five plays and even though everybody knew what was coming, they couldn't stop them.

That mentality translated on the field to "don't forget the fundamentals," but we're also going to look for new ways to teach because I think with today's kids, it's got to be a little bit new and different for them to stick with it because attention spans are not very long.

I still go to as many camps and clinics that I can, both softball and baseball, and sit and listen to learn what other people are doing. It's finding a balance between trying to be new and innovative but also keeping your hands on what has worked.

KEY POINTS FOR REVIEW:

- [ ] *Act differently than how you feel.*

- [ ] *The signs serve as great reminders for us, they're great visual cues of the thought processes that we want to have. We do a lot of daily reminders about the process.*

- [ ] *What our core covenants provide is a systematic way of saying, we want the whole package, we don't want just a winning softball team; we want good citizens, good students, good teammates, people who will give back to the community, and all the things that go into being a good human being.*

- [ ] *It's our job as coaches to use these four years to prepare them for a long and successful life after softball.*

- [ ] *When you surround yourself with good people, good things happen.*

- [ ] *We still have an underdog mentality.*

- [ ] *We want to look for new and different ways. We want to be innovative. We want to be creative. We don't want to be the "same old, same old" again because if you stand still you're going to get passed.*

- [ ] *I still go to as many camps and clinics that I can, both softball and baseball, and sit and listen to learn what other people are doing. It's finding a balance between trying to be new and innovative but also keeping your hands on what has worked.*

HOW YOU CAN BECOME A MASTER OF THE MENTAL GAME

Cain offers a range of training materials to get you or your team to the top of your game.
Available at www.BrianCain.com

MASTERS OF THE MENTAL GAME SERIES BOOKS

Champions Tell All:
Inexpensive Experience From The Worlds Best
Cain provides you with all access to some of the World's greatest performers. Learn from mixed martial arts world champions and college All-Americans about mental toughness.

The Daily Dominator:
Perform Your Best Today. Every Day!
You get 366 Daily Mental Conditioning lessons to help you start your day down the path to excellence. Investing time each day with Cain is your best way to become your best self.

The Mental Conditioning Manual:
Your Blueprint For Excellence
This is the exact system Cain uses to build champions and masters of the mental game and has helped produce NCAA and High School, champions, MMA world champions, and more.

So What, Next Pitch:
How To Play Your Best When It Means The Most
A compilation of interviews with top coaches and players where Cain teaches you their systems and tricks. Learn from the insights of these masters of the mental game.

Toilets Bricks Fish Hooks and PRIDE:
The Peak Performance Toolbox EXPOSED
Go inside the most successful programs in the country that use Cain's Peak Performance System. Use this book to unlock your potential and learn to play your best when it means the most.

MENTAL CONDITIONING & PEAK PERFORMANCE TRAINING TOOLS

Brian Cain's
Coaching The Mental Game of Softball
This is the best mental conditioning program ever created for softball coaches. Cain takes you through his entire program in four hours at the National Softball Coaches Convention with over 200 Coaches. 3 CD, 2 DVD and an over 100 page manual..

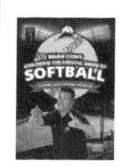

The Peak Performance System: (P.R.I.D.E.)
Personal Responsibility In Daily Excellence
This big, video-based training program is Cain's signature training program for coaches, athletes and teams. It will take you step by step to the top of the performance mountain.

Diamond Domination Training
This training program is being used by 11 teams in the NCAA top 25 in college baseball and 8 of the top 25 in college softball. It will help you and your team to unlock your potential and play the best baseball and softball of your life.

Brian Cain's Automobile University
Brian Cain's Automobile University program takes you inside of his live presentations on the mental game of softball and baseball and gives you an all access pass to Cain's material. Great coaches and athletes never stop learning and this program is key to your degree in mental game domination.

And more at www.BrianCain.com

"Brian Cain is the best mental game coach I have seen in all of my clinics/conventions I have attended over the years. OUTSTANDING!!!"

Lonni Alameda,
Head Softball Coach,
Florida State University

CONNECT WITH CAIN

Your link to doing a little a lot, not a lot a little

twitter.com/briancainpeak

facebook.com/briancainpeak

linkedin.com/in/briancainpeak

youtube.com/wwwbriancaincom

briancain.com/podcast

SIGN UP FOR BRIAN CAIN'S
WEEKLY MENTAL CONDITIONING MESSAGE

Every Monday you can hear straight from Cain with his VIP Monday Message. Send directly to your inbox, Cain's emails are full of information to help you unlock your potential and perform at your best when it means the most. Subscribe today for FREE!

www.BrianCain.com/monday

DOMINATE THE DAY!!!

WHO IS BRIAN M. CAIN, MS, CMAA – PEAK PERFORMANCE COACH

Brian M. Cain, MS, CMAA is one of the top Applied Sport Psychology and Peak Performance Coaches in the world. He is committed to helping you achieve your best when it means the most. Champions know that consistency wins and that it means the most to be at the top of their game every day.

Cain works with coaches and athletes of all levels and with corporate professionals on achieving excellence and consistent performance through Applied Sport Psychology and Peak Performance skills training.

Cain has worked with top collegiate teams on maximizing their mental game, at schools such as The University of Alabama, The University of Mississippi, The University of Tennessee, The University of Maryland, The University of Iowa, Auburn, Vanderbilt, Yale, TCU, Cal State Fullerton and many more.

He has also been in the corner with Ultimate Fighting Champions for their main event bouts and on the sideline and in the dugout at NCAA Championships. He has worked with numerous professional athletes and teams including the Washington Nationals Professional Baseball Organization.

One of the most dynamic and energetic coaches and presenters you will ever work with, Cain has addressed international audiences on a variety of topics related to Peak Performance. His custom- designed, intensive Peak Performance Bootcamps, Workshops, Seminars and Keynote Speeches have informed, inspired and edutained (educated and entertained) audiences all over the World. Visit Cain's website at www.briancain.com

to find out how you can work with Brian to help you achieve your best when it means the most.

CONCENTRATION GRIDS

39	48	59	28	71	26	34	70	95	06
21	91	42	12	30	84	76	97	61	75
58	08	85	32	45	66	36	63	23	29
96	80	00	88	89	11	25	57	02	90
74	33	56	93	52	73	04	10	49	19
87	09	16	81	69	38	64	50	83	41
31	01	40	47	18	77	24	14	13	60
79	72	05	51	82	55	15	17	44	94
54	35	53	68	65	20	03	99	86	27
67	46	07	78	22	92	37	62	98	43

39	48	59	28	71	26	34	70	95	06
21	91	42	12	30	84	76	97	61	75
58	08	85	32	45	66	36	63	23	29
96	80	00	88	89	11	25	57	02	90
74	33	56	93	52	73	04	10	49	19
87	09	16	81	69	38	64	50	83	41
31	01	40	47	18	77	24	14	13	60
79	72	05	51	82	55	15	17	44	94
54	35	53	68	65	20	03	99	86	27
67	46	07	78	22	92	37	62	98	43

39	48	59	28	71	26	34	70	95	06
21	91	42	12	30	84	76	97	61	75
58	08	85	32	45	66	36	63	23	29
96	80	00	88	89	11	25	57	02	90
74	33	56	93	52	73	04	10	49	19
87	09	16	81	69	38	64	50	83	41
31	01	40	47	18	77	24	14	13	60
79	72	05	51	82	55	15	17	44	94
54	35	53	68	65	20	03	99	86	27
67	46	07	78	22	92	37	62	98	43

39	48	59	28	71	26	34	70	95	06
21	91	42	12	30	84	76	97	61	75
58	08	85	32	45	66	36	63	23	29
96	80	00	88	89	11	25	57	02	90
74	33	56	93	52	73	04	10	49	19
87	09	16	81	69	38	64	50	83	41
31	01	40	47	18	77	24	14	13	60
79	72	05	51	82	55	15	17	44	94
54	35	53	68	65	20	03	99	86	27
67	46	07	78	22	92	37	62	98	43

39	48	59	28	71	26	34	70	95	06
21	91	42	12	30	84	76	97	61	75
58	08	85	32	45	66	36	63	23	29
96	80	00	88	89	11	25	57	02	90
74	33	56	93	52	73	04	10	49	19
87	09	16	81	69	38	64	50	83	41
31	01	40	47	18	77	24	14	13	60
79	72	05	51	82	55	15	17	44	94
54	35	53	68	65	20	03	99	86	27
67	46	07	78	22	92	37	62	98	43

39	48	59	28	71	26	34	70	95	06
21	91	42	12	30	84	76	97	61	75
58	08	85	32	45	66	36	63	23	29
96	80	00	88	89	11	25	57	02	90
74	33	56	93	52	73	04	10	49	19
87	09	16	81	69	38	64	50	83	41
31	01	40	47	18	77	24	14	13	60
79	72	05	51	82	55	15	17	44	94
54	35	53	68	65	20	03	99	86	27
67	46	07	78	22	92	37	62	98	43

39	48	59	28	71	26	34	70	95	06
21	91	42	12	30	84	76	97	61	75
58	08	85	32	45	66	36	63	23	29
96	80	00	88	89	11	25	57	02	90
74	33	56	93	52	73	04	10	49	19
87	09	16	81	69	38	64	50	83	41
31	01	40	47	18	77	24	14	13	60
79	72	05	51	82	55	15	17	44	94
54	35	53	68	65	20	03	99	86	27
67	46	07	78	22	92	37	62	98	43

39	48	59	28	71	26	34	70	95	06
21	91	42	12	30	84	76	97	61	75
58	08	85	32	45	66	36	63	23	29
96	80	00	88	89	11	25	57	02	90
74	33	56	93	52	73	04	10	49	19
87	09	16	81	69	38	64	50	83	41
31	01	40	47	18	77	24	14	13	60
79	72	05	51	82	55	15	17	44	94
54	35	53	68	65	20	03	99	86	27
67	46	07	78	22	92	37	62	98	43

39	48	59	28	71	26	34	70	95	06
21	91	42	12	30	84	76	97	61	75
58	08	85	32	45	66	36	63	23	29
96	80	00	88	89	11	25	57	02	90
74	33	56	93	52	73	04	10	49	19
87	09	16	81	69	38	64	50	83	41
31	01	40	47	18	77	24	14	13	60
79	72	05	51	82	55	15	17	44	94
54	35	53	68	65	20	03	99	86	27
67	46	07	78	22	92	37	62	98	43

39	48	59	28	71	26	34	70	95	06
21	91	42	12	30	84	76	97	61	75
58	08	85	32	45	66	36	63	23	29
96	80	00	88	89	11	25	57	02	90
74	33	56	93	52	73	04	10	49	19
87	09	16	81	69	38	64	50	83	41
31	01	40	47	18	77	24	14	13	60
79	72	05	51	82	55	15	17	44	94
54	35	53	68	65	20	03	99	86	27
67	46	07	78	22	92	37	62	98	43

39	48	59	28	71	26	34	70	95	06
21	91	42	12	30	84	76	97	61	75
58	08	85	32	45	66	36	63	23	29
96	80	00	88	89	11	25	57	02	90
74	33	56	93	52	73	04	10	49	19
87	09	16	81	69	38	64	50	83	41
31	01	40	47	18	77	24	14	13	60
79	72	05	51	82	55	15	17	44	94
54	35	53	68	65	20	03	99	86	27
67	46	07	78	22	92	37	62	98	43

39	48	59	28	71	26	34	70	95	06
21	91	42	12	30	84	76	97	61	75
58	08	85	32	45	66	36	63	23	29
96	80	00	88	89	11	25	57	02	90
74	33	56	93	52	73	04	10	49	19
87	09	16	81	69	38	64	50	83	41
31	01	40	47	18	77	24	14	13	60
79	72	05	51	82	55	15	17	44	94
54	35	53	68	65	20	03	99	86	27
67	46	07	78	22	92	37	62	98	43

39	48	59	28	71	26	34	70	95	06
21	91	42	12	30	84	76	97	61	75
58	08	85	32	45	66	36	63	23	29
96	80	00	88	89	11	25	57	02	90
74	33	56	93	52	73	04	10	49	19
87	09	16	81	69	38	64	50	83	41
31	01	40	47	18	77	24	14	13	60
79	72	05	51	82	55	15	17	44	94
54	35	53	68	65	20	03	99	86	27
67	46	07	78	22	92	37	62	98	43

39	48	59	28	71	26	34	70	95	06
21	91	42	12	30	84	76	97	61	75
58	08	85	32	45	66	36	63	23	29
96	80	00	88	89	11	25	57	02	90
74	33	56	93	52	73	04	10	49	19
87	09	16	81	69	38	64	50	83	41
31	01	40	47	18	77	24	14	13	60
79	72	05	51	82	55	15	17	44	94
54	35	53	68	65	20	03	99	86	27
67	46	07	78	22	92	37	62	98	43

www.briancain.com/softball

39	48	59	28	71	26	34	70	95	06
21	91	42	12	30	84	76	97	61	75
58	08	85	32	45	66	36	63	23	29
96	80	00	88	89	11	25	57	02	90
74	33	56	93	52	73	04	10	49	19
87	09	16	81	69	38	64	50	83	41
31	01	40	47	18	77	24	14	13	60
79	72	05	51	82	55	15	17	44	94
54	35	53	68	65	20	03	99	86	27
67	46	07	78	22	92	37	62	98	43

39	48	59	28	71	26	34	70	95	06
21	91	42	12	30	84	76	97	61	75
58	08	85	32	45	66	36	63	23	29
96	80	00	88	89	11	25	57	02	90
74	33	56	93	52	73	04	10	49	19
87	09	16	81	69	38	64	50	83	41
31	01	40	47	18	77	24	14	13	60
79	72	05	51	82	55	15	17	44	94
54	35	53	68	65	20	03	99	86	27
67	46	07	78	22	92	37	62	98	43

39	48	59	28	71	26	34	70	95	06
21	91	42	12	30	84	76	97	61	75
58	08	85	32	45	66	36	63	23	29
96	80	00	88	89	11	25	57	02	90
74	33	56	93	52	73	04	10	49	19
87	09	16	81	69	38	64	50	83	41
31	01	40	47	18	77	24	14	13	60
79	72	05	51	82	55	15	17	44	94
54	35	53	68	65	20	03	99	86	27
67	46	07	78	22	92	37	62	98	43

39	48	59	28	71	26	34	70	95	06
21	91	42	12	30	84	76	97	61	75
58	08	85	32	45	66	36	63	23	29
96	80	00	88	89	11	25	57	02	90
74	33	56	93	52	73	04	10	49	19
87	09	16	81	69	38	64	50	83	41
31	01	40	47	18	77	24	14	13	60
79	72	05	51	82	55	15	17	44	94
54	35	53	68	65	20	03	99	86	27
67	46	07	78	22	92	37	62	98	43

39	48	59	28	71	26	34	70	95	06
21	91	42	12	30	84	76	97	61	75
58	08	85	32	45	66	36	63	23	29
96	80	00	88	89	11	25	57	02	90
74	33	56	93	52	73	04	10	49	19
87	09	16	81	69	38	64	50	83	41
31	01	40	47	18	77	24	14	13	60
79	72	05	51	82	55	15	17	44	94
54	35	53	68	65	20	03	99	86	27
67	46	07	78	22	92	37	62	98	43

39	48	59	28	71	26	34	70	95	06
21	91	42	12	30	84	76	97	61	75
58	08	85	32	45	66	36	63	23	29
96	80	00	88	89	11	25	57	02	90
74	33	56	93	52	73	04	10	49	19
87	09	16	81	69	38	64	50	83	41
31	01	40	47	18	77	24	14	13	60
79	72	05	51	82	55	15	17	44	94
54	35	53	68	65	20	03	99	86	27
67	46	07	78	22	92	37	62	98	43

NOTES PAGES

3 rules of engagement
- levels 3, 5, 8 energy
- callback
- 30 sec. drill

Invest/spend
- play one pitch at a time
  give yourself the best chance
  for success
- pre practice mission/goal
  Specific
  Measurable = motivation
  A ~~scribbled~~ accountable/agressive
  Relentless
  Time

Quality at bats

I'M POSSIBLE

48 hour rule
- Goals for the week on the mirror
- energy is contagious
- If you want more, you must become more
- N.E.T = No Extra Time
- Adverse to yourself

BrianCain.com/softball
Send files
- Daily Dominant
The role of parents in highschool athletics
Attack the books
I can do anything

What do you know now you
wish you knew then.

be comfortable & uncomfortable

3 key to remember things
- location
- picture
- Give the pic a meaning

play one pitch @
a time

process/outcome
WIN = whats important
now

CAN	CANT

E + R = O

events + response = outcome

appearance = body language

confidence = action / feeling

Attitude
Perspective

{ effort
  energy
  emotion

Made in the USA
San Bernardino, CA
24 September 2014